THE CHURCH THROUGH THE AGES

BIBLE

COMMENT

THANKS

I want to thank those responsible for those responsible for the creation and publication of this work, which will certainly be of great value in the lives of Bible scholars, to considerably increase their knowledge of the Holy Scriptures. I therefore thank the Father, Son and Holy Spirit, my faithful inspirers.

AUTHOR'S FOREWORD

The church created by Jesus Christ in Jerusalem continued its mission to bring the Good News of Salvation to the world to the ends of the earth, overcoming countless obstacles and overcoming countless trials during these more than two thousand years since its founder returned to heaven.

However, despite the efforts made and the blood price paid by the Redeemer at Calvary and the first Christians, so that the opportunity of reconciliation of the sinner with God was possible for all of us, it could not remain intact and free from the contamination of evil.

The church, today, is almost completely defeated by secularism, religious modernism and the doctrine of Balaam took the place of the Gospel left by Jesus. In our day, being a Christian is to accumulate wealth in this world, freely practice immorality, pervert the good customs taught in the Scriptures and live as the infidels live. As Christ will meet his bride on the day of her coming, will she survive through the centuries to come, or will she cease to exist altogether?

SUMMARY

INTRODUCTION

The plan of salvation to rescue man from his pitiful state of sin, and allow him to be reconciled with his Creator, began even in Eden, when the woman was seduced to disobey the divine ordinances and he, for loving her more than to God, he chose to please her and also to eat of the forbidden fruit (Genesis 3:1-24) It developed at the beginning of Christ's earthly ministry and was consolidated with his death and resurrection (John 19:17-27)

Still on the cross, when he said to the father: "It is all finished". (John 19:28-30) made it clear that he fulfilled his mission as the Messiah who had to come and the role of the Lamb that takes away the sin of the world (John 1:29). The mission of the church in proclaiming the earthly kingdom of Christ began, definitively, when he ascended to heaven and his disciples began to announce the Good News of Salvation to all the lost. Beginning in Jerusalem and then spreading throughout Asia, reaching us down through the ages (Acts 12:24) All generations, from the earliest years after the resurrection of our Redeemer.

They began to hear about God's purpose in allowing man the opportunity to abandon his rebellious life and turn to a harmonious relationship between Father and Son. By adoption, through Jesus, the firstborn among all others. From the beginnings of evangelization, started with Christ and continued with the twelve apostles in Jerusalem. The gospel is freely preached to all who are willing to hear it and accept it as the only rule of faith for the salvation of their souls.

All Christians, regardless of race, color, creed or social status, are fully committed to the duty of announcing to sinners that their return to this world to take their elect is at hand, and that the condition of being saved is accepted. him as the only Lord of their lives. That your transgressions may be forgiven and lost fellowship with the father restored (Philippians 3:20).

1. THE ORIGIN OF THE CHURCH

The Christian church began to exist from the moment the Lord commissioned his first disciples to follow him (Luke 6:13), however, it was officially founded on the day of his ascent to heaven. At that exact moment, when I gave them the necessary instructions on how to act and then fulfill their evangelizing mission. the foundations of the church were laid, which at the price of many sufferings came to us. From that day and after Pentecost, when the power promised by

Christ was poured out on each of the disciples, a real battle of light against darkness began in order to free man from spiritual prisons (Acts 2:1-41) And hell did not remain silent in the face of this, on the contrary, he rose up greatly against the elect and began to use all his influence in this world to stop them (Acts 7:54-60). Lord to continue your journey towards the future and fulfill your redemptive mission, through the cross of the Savior.

There were countless attacks by enemies, many suffered the most indescribable tortures, others died burned, sawn in half, crucified, buried alive... (Hebrews 11:32-38) But all this carnage only increased the efforts of those who continued the evangelizing work, it seemed that every drop of blood shed gave rise to hundreds of new saved from evil influences.

"There was not and will not be a force that can stop the journey of the true children of God until their meeting with the bridegroom. The church founded by Jesus is grounded in his promises that the gates of hell will not...

Prevail against it (Matthew 6:18) "According to Curtis: "Perhaps Christianity would not have expanded as successfully if the Roman Empire had not existed. We can say that the Roman Empire was a gas drum waiting for the spark of Christian faith." Some of the Characteristics of the Roman Empire that contributed to the spread of the Christian faith: A certain initial religious opening, generated by the great polytheism.

The Roman population's search for the eastern beliefs that were currently on the rise; a gigantic empire reinforced by trade and sending troops to the colonies; Great diffusion of Latin and Greek as universal languages in that period. It took the Romans three decades to understand that Christianity was different from Judaism, which in those days was a legalized religion.

The Historian Tacitus before the fire already recounts conversations in tenements about a certain "Christos", certainly Christ; On July 19, 64, the fire broke out in Rome. Among the 14 blocks that had popular tenements, 10 were burned in a fire that lasted for 7 days; Christians were the scapegoat found by Nero, who swore to persecute them all to death. According to Kenneth:

"When Christianity challenged Rome's deeply ingrained polytheism, the Empire fought back."

Then there is a first wave of persecutions from 64 to 68, when Nero dies after murdering his own mother. Tacitus, a writer of that time says in one of his accounts:

"Some were dressed in the skins of wild animals and chased by dogs until they were killed, others were crucified; others wrapped in tarred cloth, and then set on fire at sunset. So, they could serve as lights to illuminate the city at night.

NERO ceded his own gardens for these executions and presented, at the same time, some circus games, witnessing the entire scene dressed as a track, sometimes walking through the crowd, sometimes watching the spectacle from his car." Second Curtis:

"In one of his first imperial acts, Vespasian appointed his son, Titus, to lead the war against the Jews. The situation turned against Jerusalem, now surrounded and isolated from the rest of the country.

Inner city factions quarreled over defense strategies. As the siege dragged on, people died of hunger and disease. The high priest's wife, once surrounded by luxury, rummaged through the city's dumpsters for food. Meanwhile, the Romans employed new war machines to hurl stones at the city walls.

ARIETES, said: "They forced the walls of the fortifications. Jewish defenders fought all day and tried to rebuild the walls at night. Finally, the Romans broke through the outer wall, then the second wall, finally reaching the third wall. The Jews, however, continued to fight as they rushed to the Temple — their last line of defense. That was the end for the brave Jewish warriors — and also for the Temple.

JOSEPH, a Jewish historian, said that Titus wanted to preserve the Temple. But the soldiers were so angry at the resistance of opponents that they ended up burning him. The fall of Jerusalem essentially ended the revolt. Jews were decimated or captured and sold into slavery.

The group of Zealots that had taken MASSADA remained in the fortress for three years. When the Romans finally built the ramp to surround and invade the site, they found all the rebels dead. They committed suicide so that they would not be captured by the invaders.

The Jewish revolt marked the end of the Jewish state, at least until modern times. The destruction of the Temple of Herod meant a change in Jewish worship.

When the Babylonians destroyed the Temple of Solomon in 586 BC, the Jews established synagogues where they could study the Law of God. The destruction of the Temple of Herod ended the Jewish sacrificial system and forced them to rely only on synagogues, which grew in importance". According to DURANT: "They met in private rooms or small chapels and organized themselves according to the synagogue model.

The congregation was called EKKLESIA - a Greek word for municipal government meetings. Slaves were welcome, as in the cults of Isis and Mithras. No attempt was made to set them free, but they comforted them with the promise of a Kingdom in which they would be set free. Among the first converts, the proletarians predominated, with some elements from the middle classes and one or another from the upper class. However, they were far from **being the "scum of society" as CELSO said.** Most of them lived industriousness, financed missions, raised funds for the poorest communities.

Little effort was made to win over the people of the countryside; the rural population came last, hence the name PAGANI (villagers, peasants) which began to be applied to the inhabitants of the Mediterranean states prior to the Christians. Congregations admitted women.

That they were in charge of small roles; but the Church demanded that they shame the heathen by the example of their lives of modest submission and recollection". — HATSENBERGER, DIONYSUS. Church History, Christianity in the Ages. "The frustrated attempts of the enemies of the gospel, in trying in every way to stop the growth of the saved in Christ, always came to nothing. From century to century their numbers only increased. Despite Satan having planted his evil seed in the field where the roots of the true wheat lie (Matthew 13: 24-30) the chosen one of the Lamb survived all the storms and strong storms that befell her.

And above all, a great comfort: Her creator, the one who built his foundations in this world, Jesus Christ, the Only Begotten of God, never forsook her nor will he forsake her. For with his bride, he will be every day, until the end of the centuries (Matthew 28:20). Notwithstanding the persecutions, martyrdoms and calumnies of the ungodly and of the tares present among the faithful, the church remained firm in its struggle for the salvation of the lost, tirelessly announcing the soon return of the Savior.

And the need for repentance on the part of unbelievers. "The history of the Church of God has always been, from the apostolic era to the present, the history of divine grace in the midst of human errors. This has been said many times, and anyone who examines this story closely cannot help but be convinced that this is so. Reading the New Testament Epistles. We see that even in apostolic times error was manifested, and that enmity, contention, anger, strife, and discord, with other evils. Had erased the love in the hearts of many true believers.

They left their first works and their first love, and some who had started with the spirit, sought after to be perfected by the flesh. But there was much more to it than that. Not only were there some true believers in whose lives many irregularities were seen, and who sought, by their words, to attract disciples to themselves, but there were also others who were not some Christians at all, but who slipped in among the brethren, sowing discord there.

This describes the state of affairs referred to in the opening verses of chapter two of Revelation, in the letter written to the angel of the church in Ephesus.

Times of Persecution

But a time of persecution for the Church was coming, and this was permitted by the Lord, in His grace, that the faithful might be distinguished.

This persecution, instigated by the Roman Emperor Nero, was the first of ten general persecutions that continued, almost without interruption, for three centuries. "Why does God allow his beloved people to suffer like this?" This question has been asked many times, and the answer is simple: it is because He loves these people. There could be, and no doubt are, other reasons, but the main one is this — He loves you.

"For the Lord corrected him that he loveth," and if the heart is led astray, discipline is needed. How easily evil binds, even to the best of men! But in the furnace of affliction, the dross separates. from the precious metal, being that which is consumed. Moreover, when we endure God's correction, He treats us as children. And if we suffer patiently, every provocation He puts us through will result in another blessing for ours. Such an experience is not pleasing to us, nor would it be a provocation if it were, but the night of sorrow follows the morning of joy, and we say with the psalmist David:

"It was good for me to have suffered affliction." Why God Allows Persecution but God sometimes allows wickedness to take man very far in persecuting Christians, in order to make manifest what is in his heart, and so, it is not surprising that in the soul of the Christian he has not appreciated this truth raises doubts and difficulties, and it begins to complain that the way is costly, and that the oppressor's hand is heavy on him.

The Lord, however, does not leave us on Earth for us to complain about the difficulties, nor to retreat from the wrath of men: We have to serve the Master and resist the enemy, but it is only when we are strengthened in the Lord and in the strength of His power that we can render this service. Or effectively resist that enemy. This story is intended to indicate how dignified this was done in times past. But if we want to understand the way God has treated his people.

We must always remember that the Christian militia is unlike any other, and that part of its resistance is suffering. The weapons of our warfare are not carnal but spiritual, and the Christian who uses fleshly weapons shows no doubt that he does not appreciate the character of the true believer.

He could not have appreciated his Lord's way with spiritual intelligence, or understood the meaning of his words: "My kingdom is not of this world; if my kingdom were of this world, my servants would fight." The militant church is a church that suffers, but if it employs carnal weapons, it actually ceases to fight." — *RINALDI, CADU. First Century of the Christian Era, blogspot.com, 2010*

Because he gave himself as an offering for our sins and, not for a moment, refused to pay the high price that was imposed on him to be rescued from our vein way of life (1 Peter 1:18)

It's up to each one of us, truly converted Christians, the commitment to continue the arduous task of proclaiming his message of salvation to those who stagger like blind men towards hell.

Let us remember the great martyrdom suffered by the Lord on that rude cross in order to allow us freedom from sin. The same as today we must address God without the intervention of anyone, through our prayers that are presented to the Father through the Son, in whom we are united through faith (John 17:21)

All the suffering of Christ on the tree was only to conquer our rapprochement with the Creator, from whom we were forced to distance ourselves due to the existence of sin. And when he said, at the moment of his death:

"It is all finished!", it confirmed our release from the shackles of death". We don't need to think too much of that since we were living in our sins and always offending God with our iniquities. It follows that we were enemies of God.

So, if we were God's enemies. Soon, we would need to be reconciled. The truth is, Christ's death ends the enmity between God and man. Our hostility to God was removed by the blood of Christ on the cross. In Romans 5:10 it says, "we have been reconciled to God." How do we achieve this reconciliation? Through Jesus' death. Note that this act of reconciliation was not our initiative, but exclusively God's. Despite being his enemies, He was always our friend, to the point of sending His own and only Son to die for us, with the purpose of restoring the fellowship we had lost with Adam's disobedience.

A very significant passage is Romans 11:15. World reconciliation is now possible because the Jews rejected the Messiah. Note that in rejecting the Jews, God takes the initiative, withdrawing from Israel the divine favor and grace of the gospel. The reconciliation of the world (Gentiles) stands in contrast to the rejection of Israel. Therefore, it is assumed that reconciliation is an act of God, his act of receiving the world in his favor and dealing with it in a special way. Important: As important as turning to God is, the reconciliation process is God returning to us with his favor.

That's wonderful. In addition to God saving us, He also restores lost fellowship. From enemies we become friends of God. Christ's death was sacrificial, and since it was a sacrifice, it was also propitiatory, in the sense that it satisfied all of God's requirements. It was also a substitute; his death was in our place.

It was an undeserved favor from God – to send his Son to die for us. And ultimately reconciling, Christ's death made us God's friends. In conclusion, Christ's death is the best gift we could ever receive at the hands of God.

"For the gift of God is eternal life in Jesus Christ our Lord" *V. MILLARD J. ERICKSON. Systematic Theology — LEE, CARLOS — Learning from the Scriptures, 2011*

2 – THE CHURCH'S MISSION: EVANGELIZATION

J ust as the Lord ascended into heaven, in front of the eyes of his disciples who remained faithful to the new faith received, his last recommendation was that they remain waiting until power was sent to them from heaven, after which they should go out to proclaim the gospel to every creature, serving him as witnesses in Jerusalem, in Judea, and to the ends of the earth. (Acts 1:8) The primary mission of the church of Christ is to proclaim the Gospel.

Incessantly, so that man may repent of his evil ways and return to lost communion with his Creator. And it is only through evangelization that it will be able to achieve positive results in this regard. If Christians are not willing to go out into the streets, alleys and ditches (Luke 14:21)

In search of the lost, in order to tell them about the immense love of God and the plan of salvation that he designed, through his Son Jesus, to rescue them from the clutches of the evil one, they will not be fulfilling their part as a member of the body of Christ.

And therefore, they fail as messengers of the kingdom, a function for which they have been commissioned by the Lord of all the earth. To be a Christian means to be saved by the faith placed in the Only Begotten of the Father and, therefore, to be committed to the mission of bringing to those who are still lost the revelation of the Savior's sacrifice on the cross.

For all to come to full knowledge and be saved (1 Timothy 2:4) Believers who do not evangelize are branches that are not bearing fruit and will eventually be cut off and the end will be wither and die (John 1-6) In our temples, what else exists are pastors and workers of all kinds dressed in their beautiful suits, accommodated in luxurious cabinets and armchairs.

Without giving a damn for the souls that die every second that passes in the hands of Satan, who uses violence, drugs, prostitution and everything that causes physical, moral and spiritual destruction, to annihilate once and for all the main creation of God, man. In fact, most of those who call themselves "Christians" are nothing but wolves camouflaged in sheep's clothing.

Seeking to satisfy their material greed, gain fame and popular recognition. There are many who make use of social networks to publish videos with preaching and prophecies of the flesh, one competing with the other publicly, claiming to be evangelizing the unbelievers, when in reality what they manage is to create scandals for the name of the church and the Lord (Matthew 18:7) Jesus showed the right way to evangelize himself, taking care to avoid sensationalism, personal marketing, and exaltation.

He became the greatest preacher in the history of mankind, he was special and admirable in everything he did during his ministry, however, as described by the messianic prophet centuries before he came to this world, he was a simple man, without physical beauty and nothing that Deserving Admiration (Isaiah 53:2) However, what is seen in the pulpits today are disputes between workers. To see who wears the best suit, the sisters spend what they cannot to parade with their expensive dresses and show the economic power they have, in front of the less favored, forgetting the warning of the Spirit of God to the churches, through Paul, who warns for the daughters of God to dress simply.

The Church Through the Ages

Without false modesty, neither wearing expensive jewelry nor make-up, as saints must do (1 Timothy 2:9) And while materialistic disputes increase, he forgets to take the Gospel to the captives of the evil one. And these remain chained to the Devil's chains, without any hope of seeing the light dawn. But the Lord's warning for this neglect is serious and at the right time he will charge each one for the fruits they should bear, and they will not present anything, on that day of reckoning (Matthew 25:14-30)

If the bride of Christ, who is his greatest representative in this world, not fully fulfill his duty to propagate to the four corners of the earth that he will soon come and give to each according to his works (Revelation 2:23) Mankind will follow blindly towards the abyss that lies open right in front of him, and the blood of those who have gone astray without being warned of the danger, will be upon his head (Ezekiel 33:8)

We are all Watchtowers of Christ and as such we have the duty to climb the highest mountain and lift up our voice strongly, announcing the coming of the Lord to the unnoticed who walk asleep by sin, completely ignorant of the truths of God. If the sinner stumbles in his own transgressions, falls and dies spiritually (Ezekiel 3:20) the fault will be entirely ours, for we keep our lips closed without warning him of the evil that befell him.

Few Christians today stop to think about how critical the situation will be for those who, after receiving freely from the Lord the salvation and forgiveness of their sins, act in a selfish way. Enjoying God's mercy. Refusing to go after their brothers who are still in darkness, so that they, too, can be freed and saved, they are like a fig tree that, for not bearing its fruit, will wither and lose eternal life (Matthew 21:18- 22). The responsibility of the church to evangelize more and more, now that the day of the end approaches, the hour of Christ's return and the final judgment, is immense.

It's so great that if we don't do this million and millions of souls will be thrown into the lake of fire along with Satan and his demons, all because we were negligent in our mission to evangelize. Regarding this important task that the Lord Jesus Christ commissioned the entire church, Pastor David Hatcher, thus commented in one of his sermons: "The reason we Christians are on earth is because of God. Therefore, we need to be better examples, correct in our behavior and in our service. God's cause is to bring His Kingdom to earth.

This is our mission: to speak and show the gospel to as many people as possible. God's will is that all men should be saved. And people can only be saved if they know the gospel. There are many things being said about the gospel, but without effect, because in some cases the explanation lacks clarity. So, let's take a simple approach to speaking and presenting the gospel to people through evangelistic design. You can follow along with the drawing at the end of this summary.

1st – Start by drawing a triangle that represents the trinity of God the Father, Son and the Holy Spirit and identify it with the letter "D". Then place in each angle the main qualities of God "Almighty", "Love", "Holy". **2° – Start talking about the creation of the earth and of the man: God created the heavens and the earth and everything that exists. He created man, male and female, to have a relationship with him, and he loved so much that he gave free will.**

Because love does not force. Acts 17:24-27: "The God who made the world and all that is in it is the Lord of heaven and earth, and he does not dwell in sanctuaries made by human hands. He is not served by the hands of men, as if he needed something, because he himself gives everyone life, breath and other things. He made all the peoples out of one, so that they might populate the whole earth, having determined the times previously established and the exact places in which they should dwell.

God did this so that men would seek him and perhaps, groping, they might find him, although he is not far from each of us." 3rd – But man did not want to obey God and preferred to follow his own heart. By man's sin he was cut off from God's presence and cut off in His spirit. With that, sin and death came into the world. – Draw on the side an inverted star representing Satan and identify it with an "S" – Then, the man far from the presence of God began to live and die under the influence of Satan.

4th – The composition of our being, we are: Body, Soul and Spirit.

• Body: Physical, visible, mortal.

• Soul: Thought, will, will.

• Spirit: Breath of life through which we reconnect with God, eternal.

5th – When Adam and Eve sinned, they disconnected from God in the Spirit, and sin and death came. You and I were born disconnected from God and in sin, but God, in his infinite mercy and infinite love for us, began to outline the Plan of Salvation by which we would be reconnected to Him. with the birth of Jesus Christ, about 2000 years ago, the Lamb of God who takes away the sin of the world.

1st Timothy 2:5: "For there is one God and one mediator between God and men: the man Christ Jesus" 6th – Jesus was born of the Virgin Mary, so he was not conceived in sin, but by the Holy Spirit. He came into the world 100% man and 100% God, with the perfect Spirit directly linked to the Father. It was then through his delivery on the cross of Calvary that the door was opened for us to return to God. By the work of Jesus Christ who died for our sin. Romans 5:7-11: "There is hardly anyone to die for a righteous man; for the good man maybe, someone has the courage to die. But God demonstrates his love for us:

Christ died for us while we were still sinners. As we are now justified by his blood, how much more will we be saved from the wrath of God through him! If when we were God's enemies, we were reconciled to him through the death of his Son, how much more so now, having been reconciled.

We will be saved for your life! Not only that, but we also glory in God, through our Lord Jesus Christ, through whom we have now received reconciliation." Hebrews 12:2: "with an eye single to Jesus, the author and finisher of our faith. He, for the joy that had been set before him, endured the cross, despising shame, and sat at the right hand of the throne of God."

7th – Will everyone be saved? Unfortunately, not. But everyone can be saved! All who confess Jesus Christ as Lord of their life and believe in his work on the cross and that God raised him on the third day. Romans 10:9: "If you confess with your mouth that Jesus is Lord and believe in your heart that God raised him from the dead, you will be saved."

Then instantly the Holy Spirit of God comes and reconnects with you, and you receive eternal life. Will be ready to receive the gifts of God, the rewards.

John 1:12: "But to those who received him, to those who believed in his name, he gave the right to become children of God"

Ephesians 1: 5-8: "In love he predestined us to be adopted as children through Jesus Christ, according to the good purpose of his will, to the praise of his glorious grace, which he freely gave us in the Beloved. In him we have redemption through his blood, the forgiveness of sins.

According to the riches of God's grace, which he bestowed upon us with all wisdom and understanding."

Have you decided? Do you want?

If the person accepts Jesus Christ, Amen. Talk about the Church, not just our church, but others as well. If the person does not accept it, keep praying for him, as he is also loved by God." *Evangelize – this is our mission! God bless you! — HATCHER, DAVID. Evangelization. New Baptist Church, Manaus, 2015*

2.2 Giving Good Testimony

It is crucial for the church that identifies itself as the bride of the Lamb to show a good testimony before skeptics, especially those who insist on looking for flaws in the lives of Christians in order to criticize the faith they profess in a superior Being in which they do not believe they exist.

Faced with such modernity" that most people believe they have reached, and with that they believe they do not need salvation. An almost insurmountable spiritual barrier is created, due to their unbelief.

For the Scriptures affirm that the natural man does not understand the things of God (1 Corinthians 2:14) And, with this, they decisively refuse to listen to the preaching of the Gospel.

And if those who announce the plan of salvation through Jesus Christ do not set good examples as a Christian, then it will be much more difficult to get their attention (1 Timothy 3:7)

Decades ago, the respect that unbelievers had for evangelicals was notorious, including in relation to Pentecostals, due to their orthodox way of living the gospel, completely denying worldly customs, such as: Wearing jewelry, makeup, female haircuts and the use of clothes considered extravagant. Over the years and the loss of the fear of God for the new generation of elect, we reached the chaotic point of no longer knowing who is an atheist or a Christian.

25

Everything became a homogeneous mixture without any definition. Pastors surrendered to the new customs, claiming that if they pushed too hard, they would lose the flock to another religious denomination. And, as these days what matters is quantity and not quality, they prefer to let them live at their leisure than to see their temples empty. However, these week in faith forget that the Lord is not interested in numbers but in the holiness of the believer.

He made this very clear, when speaking sharply he was abandoned by the crowd. With only the twelve remaining, he asked them if they were not interested in leaving him too (John 6:66-68). He knew who was in fact truly following him, incited the anger of the crowd so that it would disperse, because he understood that the vast majority were only interested in his miracles.

And in the bread, he gave them. Today is no different. Crowds fill the temples of the great churches in this country, but not looking for salvation. They want nothing serious with God, nor are they willing to put into practice their ordinances described in the Holy Scriptures. As in Jesus' times, these false believers are only after the blessings and divine healings. They forget that it is the fear of the Lord that guarantees us every victory and blessing (Proverbs 19:23).

"Ye are our letter, written in our hearts, known and read by all men" (2 Cor 3:2) I once heard from the famous Jewish Rabbi that more than a messenger from God he sought to be the letter of God on this earth. I found this statement interesting, because I believe that this person never had the opportunity to read (because he is a religious of the law). And the apostle speaks exactly that, to be the letter of God here on Earth. Many Christians do not understand that more than talking about Jesus it is necessary to live Jesus. The word of God says: As ye have therefore received the Lord Jesus Christ, so walk in him also (Col 2:6) He who says that he is in him must also walk as he walked (1 John 2:6).

More than talking about the gospel, it is essential that we live the gospel of Grace. The Holy Scriptures show us that more than God's messengers, we need to be God's living letter to men. Through this, it is necessary to emphasize to every believer the importance of Christian witness. In many passages the Lord shows us how much it is necessary for us to be a witness. A testimony is the declaration of a witness and it is also a divine teaching given by God, just as a testimony is the declaration of one who has seen and heard.

That is, the reported experience of someone or something, we are in Christ as a letter to God to this world, written by the Spirit of God. The apostle Paul declares: For it is already manifest that you are the letter of Christ, ministered to us, and written, not with ink, but with the Spirit of the living God, not on tables of stone, but on the tables of flesh of the heart (2 Color 3:3). Paul was saying that a believer's greatest letter of recommendation is his Christian witness.

There are many churches that use a letter of recommendation to welcome new members. But what many letters of recommendation may lack is the veracity of a person's facts, thus resembling many of those falsified resumes that companies receive. The apostle Paul said that he did not trade the word of God, that is, he falsified as many "teachers" of the Law did.

He said that in Christ he spoke, in his presence, with sincerity and with due propriety. (2 Cor 2:17) There are many people who speak of Christ, but not sincerely, for they falsified the word of God. By the way, the origin of the Greek word for market is καπηλεύοντες = kapeléuo (gr) which denotes adulteration. Many traveling salesmen mixed water with wine to deceive their customers and customers. This word also means to corrupt. Paul said that there were many disorderly (insubordinate), vain talkers and Deceivers who taught out of filthy greed (Tit 1:10-11) There are many in the Christian milieu who do not mind being a witness of Christ.

In being a letter from God, because his life comes down to personal marketing of himself, in his own glory. It doesn't matter to them if the Christian witness they live is outside the biblical standards, the important thing is "to serve God". But what many fails to see in the heart seared by greed is that the God they serve is Mammon.

As Paul says: ..., whose god is his own womb, his glory is to their own confusion and their end is their perdition (Phil. 3:19). They only think about earthly things. And this I speak of both leaders and believers in general.

Dear ones, how can we identify who has a good Christian witness and is a letter from God? In the second part of this study, we will show by the word of God some principles for a good Christian witness.

But we can say that everyone who speaks with his life (thinking and acting) who lives according to the biblical principles of justice and righteousness, who loves his brother without pretense and who above all produces good fruit (seen so many by the brothers themselves as by non-believers)

This can be considered a good Christian witness. All things are pure to the pure, but nothing is pure to the defiled and unfaithful; rather your understanding and conscience are contaminated. They confess that they know God, but they deny him with works, being abominable, and disobedient, and reproving for every good work. (Tt 1;15-16).

But beware of false prophets, who come to you in sheep's clothing, but inwardly they are ravening wolves. By their fruits you will know them.

Do you gather grapes from thorns, or figs from thistles? So, every good tree bears good fruit, and every bad tree bears bad fruit. The good tree cannot bear bad fruit; nor does the bad tree bear good fruit. Every tree that does not bear good fruit is cut down and thrown into the fire.

Therefore, by their fruits ye shall know them. Not everything that says to me: Lord, Lord! he will enter into the kingdom of heaven, but he who does the will of my Father who is in heaven". (Mt 7:15-21) — **GOSPEL MORE. God's Letter —The Importance of Christian Witness, part 1, 2011**

2.3 Staying Santa

Nothing shames the name of God and hurts the holiness of the Holy Spirit more than the scandals caused by many Christians today in our churches.

Secular customs invaded evangelical temples and were well accepted by our young people and teenagers who, often growing up without a disorderly home, where parents do not give any witness, even if they call themselves Christians, become rebellious about the dictates of the rules of sanctity exposed in the Word of God and choose to follow in the footsteps of those who still live-in darkness.

Worst of all are certain religions, so-called modernists, which allow them the freedom to do whatever they find convenient, whose leaders are equally true tares and increasingly inflame in this rebellious youth the accursed desire to practice the sinful acts of unbelievers, claiming that Jesus will not take their youthful attitudes seriously because he is love and will always forgive them.

Faced with such spiritual disgrace, he forgets the advice given to us by wise King Solomon, in his book Ecclesiastes (Preacher), regarding the acts performed by man as a young man (Ecclesiastes 12: 1-8). We are free to live as we see fit.

God will never prevent anyone from choosing their path in this life, not least because he has given us the free will to decide to walk according to his advice or not (Jeremiah 7:24) However, as we already know, every action generates a reaction, and every transgression brings serious consequences to the transgressor. What a man sows, this very he will reap (Galatians 6:7).

The fact that the Lord is a merciful God does not mean, in the least, that He will tolerate our acts of rebellion without giving us due punishment (Proverbs 11:31). be reached by all Christians, and in all areas.

It is not enough to just leave aside some habits that are visible to those who observe us, such as vices and apparent customs. God demands complete holiness, which comes from the inside out.

A true transformation of the "inner man", that being who lives deep inside and who for years felt comfortable living under the dominion of sin. T

here are crazes and disgusting habits that even seeming harmless are intolerant of the Holy Spirit, a great example of this is the lie (John 8:44), excessive criticism (Matthew 7:1) the hasty judgment (James 4:11), murmuring (1 Corinthians 10:10), and several other things considered minimal, but which before God are absurdly unacceptable.

One of the practices that most impede the sanctification of the church in this century, full of "modern concepts", is sexual sins. Countless are those who, even after accepting Christ and already enjoying the pleasure of freedom, return to the vomit and mire of sin (2 Peter 2:22)

And, there, their spiritual state becomes seven times worse than it was before (Matthew 12:43-45) Returning to the practice of old sinful habits, especially those related to prostitution. Many who have fallen into this weakness, wonder what to do to keep themselves pure, without stumbling or returning to the old ways of the time when they were slaves of the Devil.

The psalmist advises the young person (or the whole church) to continually feed on the Holy Word of God. It will keep the Christian in full communion with the Lord and this will strengthen him against temptation (Psalm 119:9).

But in addition to reading the Bible daily and constantly seeking the presence of the Holy Spirit through prayer and fasting, there are other basic things that contribute to achieving this goal. Mark Driscoll, in his work "Sexual Sin", tells us what to do after a possible stumbling block in this type of sin: "Repent quickly and keep fighting. When you sin, repent. Ask forgiveness from God, your spouse, your accountability Christian friends, your small group, quickly. Don't let time pass. You will go into more sin, shame, condemnation and demonic accusation.

And you will begin to legitimize your sin. It will get worse. Repent quickly. Get back to Jesus quickly. Tell others the truth quickly and fight continuously. Peter says that we have desires that are at war with our soul. Paul says that our fight is not just against flesh and blood. It's not just a sexual issue. We are fighting powers, principalities and spirits.

That Satan and his demons are behind it all, and that they are actually baiting nakedness, lust and pleasures that are illegal and inappropriate. And Satan wants us to take the bait and neglect the truth that there is a hook, and we are going to be tangled up in death. It's a real fight. And so, we must continually fight." *— MARK DISCROLL. Sexual Sin. Private Hermeneutics, Synopsis, São Paulo, 2010.*

According to Mark Driscoll, the sin of lust (sexual), as well as any other that leads man to distance himself from God, comes from Satan, our greatest enemy, who makes use of our weaknesses and leads us to the spiritual abyss. And, according to their Christian point of view, the best way to resist this type of temptation is to confess the mistake made as soon as possible, because then the adversary of our souls will be prevented from emotionally blackmailing us, making us feel guilty for the mistake made. And, leading us to flee from living with our brothers and sisters in the faith, leaving the church and deviating from the path where Christ has placed us. But regardless of what the sin may be and its source.

The duty of every Christian is to strive daily to avoid voluntary practice. It must first of all reject all kinds of sin, for the Bride of Christ must be holy, pure and undefiled (Philippians 4:8). Holiness is the basis of true communion with God, without it it is impossible for the Christian to keep himself in his face. The writer to the Hebrews emphasizes that without her no one will see the Highest (Hebrews 12:14) for the glory of the Lord is so sublime that any stain of disobedience on the part of his people is an affront to him. For he is enthroned among the cherubim who day and night exalt his greatness.

(Isaiah 6:1-3). The church must indeed be formed of a people bought and redeemed in the blood of the lamb (Titus 2:14) And not colluded with worldly customs, inclined to secular habits, nor moved by the infamy of those who deny the existence of divine justice. For great will be the vengeance upon those who mock the Lord's threats against the lovers of the pleasures of this world, who doubt his vengeance and live absolute without fearing the day of his great wrath.

"Finally, brethren, we beseech you and exhort you in the Lord Jesus, that just as you have received from us, in what way it is fitting to walk and please God, so walk, that you may progress more and more. For you know well what commandments we have given you by the Lord Jesus. For this is the will of God, your sanctification; to abstain from fornication; may each of you know how to possess his vessel in sanctification and honor; not in the passion of lust, like the Gentiles, who do not know God.

Let no one oppress or deceive his brother in any business, because the Lord is the avenger of all these things, as also we have told you and testified to you before. Because God did not call us to uncleanness, but to sanctification. Therefore, whoever despises this does not despise man, but God, who also gave us his Holy Spirit." (1 Thessalonians 4:1-8) Many "woes" are reserved for the enemies of the Almighty.

The Church Through the Ages

When the end finally comes and the elect church is removed from their midst, their pains will be matchless and lovers of pleasure and sin will groan bitterly the pain of their rebellions. The chosen one, however, will be enjoying eternal rest beside her Beloved in the heavenly paradise, because she loves him and is also loved by him, because she kept her fidelity firm until the day of her rescue. This is the Lord's promise to his church, to the redeemed, to all who confess his name.

To the skeptics, however, who remain unbelieving before the warnings given by the ministers of the kingdom, to these will be reserved the fear of darkness and the fire that will never go out and will burn forever (Revelation 20:14,15) "Woe to those who pull iniquity with the ropes of vanity, and sin with the strings of a car! And they say, make haste, and finish your work, that we may see it; and come near and come the counsel of the Holy One of Israel, that we may know him. Woe to those who call evil good, and good evil; who make darkness light, and light darkness; and make the bitter sweet, and the sweet bitter!

Woe to them that are wise in their own eyes, and prudent in their own eyes! Woe to them that are mighty to drink wine, and men of might to mix strong drink. Of those who justify the ungodly by bribery, and the righteous deny justice! Therefore, as the tongue of fire consumes the straw, and the stubble dissolves by the flame.

So, will its root be like rottenness, and its flower will fade like dust; because they rejected the law of the Lord of hosts, and despised the word of the Holy One of Israel" (Isaiah 5:18-24) Those who think they are hidden from the penetrating gaze of God are deceived, for nothing will be hidden from him (Hebrews 4: 13). There is an urgent need for all Christians to live in constant vigilance. For we do not know for sure the day of his coming (Mark 13:35) And all who are not watching, with their lamps lit will be left behind (Matthew 25:1-13) There are different religious denominations spread all over the globe.

That announce the message of salvation left to us by the Son of God, in different languages, to all peoples. Both from close up and also from afar. Since the advent of technology, there are no longer any limits where the seed of the Gospel can be spread. Even in Islamic countries, considered impenetrable by Christians, it is possible to speak of the sacrifice made by our Savior in favor of the captives of Satan and some have even converted.

However, despite the enormous advance this brings us in the task of winning souls for the kingdom, it is no guarantee that we are already separated to participate in the marriage of the Lamb. That special day is reserved for a people with unusual qualities. Christ's symbolic marriage to his beloved church will be the greatest of all events that will take place in heaven until that great day, and only those with their garments completely clean will have the right to be present there, on that unique occasion (Revelation 3: 4;19:9)

Catholicism teaches its believers that Christian holiness is entirely linked to charity and a life of chastity, that penance and the rejection of marriage is the true synonym of "being holy". But this is not what the Holy Scriptures teach us. Since God commissioned Moses to bring his people out of slavery in Egypt and into the promised land, his greatest demand was that he warns them of the need to stay away from the practices used by the inhabitants of Canaan.

Place where they would be taken, so that they would not end up being contaminated with their false gods and their bad habits. (Leviticus 18: 1-3) That is, the holiness of the church, in the full biblical sense, is totally related to involvement with the immoral acts committed by the secular world around us. In the likeness of the times of Israel, where the surrounding peoples prostituted themselves, worshiped demons, lived in order to satisfy the pleasures of the flesh and not the spirit, were enslaved by sin, ignored God and had darkness as their home.

They did not dwell in the light, the people of this age also live in complete spiritual darkness and the church's duty is to act as Jesus did, to announce salvation to them, but to keep to the margins of their sinful habits. If to be saints it was enough just to be merciful to our fellow men (without denying the importance of this), to do good works and to avoid marriage, then holiness would be an extremely easy achievement.

However, what the Word of God reveals to us is that in order to be holy, man needs, before anything else, to abstain from any and all appearance of evil. Holiness means turning completely to God. Turn your back on the world and its iniquities. The modern way in which certain religions expose the concept of sanctification leads many Christians to the exaggeration of living twice as far as their Christian conduct is concerned.

The first is to think that God has modernized himself in such a way that he easily accepts sin. And the idea that the church, having to coexist with sinners in this world, has a duty to align itself with their way of life. Even if it means adapting to their immoral and disgusting customs. The second is that having already converted to Christianity, being part of a certain religion and professing the name of Christ, guarantees them a right place in the Kingdom of God.

Which is huge nonsense. The expression: Seek sanctification, without which no one will see God" (Hebrews 12:14) makes it clear that whoever does not give up the life of sin, in all its forms, will never enter paradise. Never mind the modernist concepts of pagan religions, which try to change biblical concepts at will.

2.3.1 Biblical Concepts About Holiness

Paul, servant of Christ, was decisive about the correct way in which the Christian must keep himself holy in the presence of God, in all his letters written and sent to the brothers of different churches.

Which he founded or visited during his travels. missionaries. And, for reasons beyond his will, he kept himself from speaking to them personally (Ephesians 1: 15, 16) According to the guidance given to him by the Holy Spirit, from whom he received in abundance from Christ to perfectly exercise his Ministry. He clarified to distant brethren their doubts about this important need for them to remain pure.

Abandoning any and all customs previously practiced, while living in ignorance of sin. In the fourth chapter of his letter to the believers in Ephesus, the apostle earnestly asks the church to permanently abandon its old habits, sanctifying itself in the practice of a new and different way of living: "And I say this, and I testify in the Lord, to that you no longer walk as other Gentiles walk, in the vanity of their minds.

Darkened in understanding, separated from the life of God by the ignorance that is in them, by the hardness of their heart. Who, having lost all feeling, gave themselves up to dissolution, to greedily commit all impurity? But you did not learn Christ thus, if you have heard him, and were taught in him, as is the truth in Jesus. That, as to the past deal, you divest yourselves of the old man, who is corrupted by the lusts of deceit.

And be renewed in the spirit of your mind, and put on the new man, who according to God is created in true righteousness and holiness. Therefore, leave the lie, and speak the truth, each one with his neighbor; because we are members of each other. Be angry, and do not sin; do not let the sun go down on your wrath. Do not make room for the devil. He who stole, steal no more; before he works, doing what is good with his hands, so that he has something to share with what he needs. Do not let any unwholesome word come out of your mouth, but only that which is good to promote edification, so that it gives grace to those who hear it. And grieve not the Holy Spirit of God.

In whom you are sealed for the day of redemption. All bitterness, and wrath, and wrath, and shouting, and blasphemy, and all malice be put away from among you, but be kind to one another, merciful, forgiving one another, as God also forgave you in Christ (Ephesians 4:13-32)" As he guides us, man, when approaching Christ and being enlightened by him, must live in newness of life.

Abandoning their old ways in exchange for an existence based on love for others, forgiveness of enemies, rejection of carnal desires, contempt for immorality and turning away from strife and putting off the old man, renewing itself day after day in the Spirit of God's Grace. Only those who are willing to leave behind their conceived roots in the heritage of darkness will be able to walk with Jesus toward the land he promised.

To the saved, the New Jerusalem, the Holy City that John envisioned during the revelation received from the Apocalypse, which on that Great Day will descend from heaven adorned with all the rarest precious stones to be inhabited on earth by the Lord and His Bride (Revelation 21:9 -27) For in it only those who have purified their garments in the blood of the Lamb will dwell. Therefore, Paul was reluctant to ask the church to sanctify itself:

"But fornication, and all uncleanness or greed, let it not even be named among you, the befits saints. No petty things, no nonsense, no shocking things, which are not convenient; but rather thanksgiving. For this you well know: that no lecher, or unclean, or miser, who is an idolater, has an inheritance in the kingdom of Christ and of God. for by these things the wrath of God cometh upon the children of disobedience. Therefore, do not be his companions. For at one time, you were darkness, but now you are light in the Lord; walk as children of light (For the fruit of the Spirit is in all goodness and righteousness and truth); Approving what is pleasing to the Lord.

And do not communicate with the unfruitful works of darkness, but rather condemn them. Because what they do in secret until they say it is clumsy. But all these things manifest, being condemned by the light, because the light manifests everything. Therefore, he says: Awake, you who sleep, and rise from the dead, and Christ will enlighten you. Therefore, see prudently how you walk, not as fools, but as wise, redeeming the time; because the days are bad. So don't be foolish, but understand what the Lord's will is.

And be not drunk with wine, in which there is contention, but be filled with the Spirit; Speaking to one another in psalms, and hymns, and spiritual songs; singing and singing to the Lord in your heart. Always giving thanks to put everything to our God and Father, in the name of our Lord Jesus Christ; subjecting one to you (Ephesians 5:3-21)" One of the most common sins practiced by modern society in our days after prostitution is fornication. Most Christians don't even understand the difference between one thing and another. And the biggest culprits of this moral ignorance in the church are religious leaders. Because they are more concerned with increasing membership in their temples to raise more tithes and offerings to fill their coffers.

And they forget or care little about guiding Christians about the sin of having an intimate relationship with a partner without being properly married. Fornicators and prostitutes, (which is actually the same as impure and immoral), will stay outside the Holy City. Jesus, at the end of the revelation of the End Times to John, through his angel concluded, saying:

"Blessed is he who washes his garments in the Blood of the Lamb, that he may have a right to the tree of life and enter the city through the gates. Outside will be the dogs, the sorcerers, the unclean, the murderers, the idolaters and all those who love and practice the lie" (Revelation 22:14,15)

This affirmation of Christ should serve as a warning to every Christian in an age where human laws support every kind of sin practiced by man and the skeptical society of which all of us, who inevitably belong, see everything as something natural and acceptable. Whether it be prostitution, fornication, adultery and homosexuality... Everything is seen and accepted with the greatest naturalness by everyone, big and small, rich and poor, even by a good part of those who call themselves children of God.

The truth is that, with the arrival of such religious modernism, the Christians of this century decided to follow the customs of unbelievers, some to be accepted in the environment where they live, at work and at school; others to keep their temples always full and their accounts high up.

But Paul, used by the Holy Spirit, more than two thousand years ago already warned the church of his time about the spirit of apostasy that would arise in the present day (1 Timothy 4:1-5) According to the apostle, holiness The church is not limited to avoiding illicit sexual practices, as determined by certain religions, but to any attitude directly similar to that made by the world without God.

 Even foolish words uttered thoughtlessly or purposefully, as a willful sin. Anger, bitterness, anger, fighting and gluttony, which is the habit of overeating, putting more emphasis on satisfying the physical body than the spirit, with fasting and prayer: each with his neighbor; because we are members of each other. Be angry, and do not sin; do not let the sun go down on your wrath. Do not make room for the devil. He who stole, steal no more; before he works, doing what is good with his hands, so that he has something to share with what he needs. Do not let any unwholesome word come out of your mouth, but only that which is good to promote edification, so that it gives grace to those who hear it. And grieve not the Holy Spirit of God, in whom you are sealed for the day of redemption.

All bitterness, and anger, and wrath, and shouting, and blasphemy, and all malice, be removed from among you. Rather be kind to one another, merciful, forgiving one another, as God also forgave you in Christ". (Ephesians 4:25-32)

2.4 Staying Faithful

Faithfulness must always be the foremost and greatest of all qualities in the church of Christ, after holiness. It is through it that the Christian is able to withstand the most intense trials that will arise on the way to heaven and it was because of this important condition that our brothers who lived in remote times of Christianity, were tortured and killed without, however, to deny the trust they once placed in their Savior.

All the apostles constituted in the New Testament by Jesus were put to death for refusing to curse the name of their Master or for denying their belief in him. And along with those heroes of the faith, thousands of other Christians were tortured and killed in the name of the Gospel.

However, being faithful is not a condition sought by all who convert and become part of the Christian community. As the Lord predicted, Satan planted the seed of tares in the field and he lives among the faithful, causing scandals and staining the name of the church.

However, the advice left by Peter in his first letter, written to Jewish Christians who were expelled from Jerusalem. "During the persecution of Nero, the Roman emperor who started the hunt for Christians, in AD 64, it was that they did not lose faith in the Lord,

But that they remained confident that he would never abandon them, and if that happened to the point. of being captured and killed. They would receive eternal life as a reward:

40

"Beginning in Jerusalem, the persecution spread throughout the rest of the ancient world, wherever Christians gathered. This situation reached its climax when Rome determined to rid the empire of those who "were of Christ" — those who did not bow to Caesar. Peter knew the persecution well. Beaten and imprisoned, he had been frequently threatened. he saw his fellow Christians die and the church dispersed. But he knew Christ and nothing could shake his confidence in his risen Lord.

Then he wrote to the scattered church, which was suffering for the faith, offering them comfort and hope, and exhorting them to continual loyalty to Christ" . . .— *PERSONAL APPLICATION BIBLE. Comment on Pedro, CPAD, Rio de Janeiro, p1761, 2004*

2.4.1 Job's Example

"The Word of God makes it clear that there is no one to escape the perplexities of this life (John 16:33). Even the most selfless and dedicated servants of God face crises and setbacks (Ps 55:1-6). In this lesson, Job will serve us as an archetype of faithfulness. We will learn from his overwhelming experience that the just, even in situations of crisis, must remain faithful to the Lord (Job 1:22; Hc 3:17-18).

a) Faithful Even If Relationships Are Affected.

Faith must triumph over all matters of life. Human existence is made up of interpersonal relationships in which we may suffer accusations or even indifference from those who are part of our inner circle.

b) Family Intolerance — In life's most critical situations, what we least need is someone to aggravate our anguish. In these moments, the family must become our "ground"; but this is not always the case, as was the case with Job. His home, the world of his caresses, was affected.

Even in his fidelity, faced with the tragic events, he did not find in his wife the word he so needed in that critical period of his life. But still, he remained faithful (Job 2:8-10; 19:14a). His example inspires us to remain steadfast in our faithfulness to God. Even when we do not find the long-awaited support within our family. The Scriptures reveal to us that even Jesus, our greatest inspiration, suffered misunderstandings from His family (Mark 3:31, 32).

c) The accusations of friends.

One of the lessons we learn, when inserted in adversity, is to identify who our true friends are (Prov 17:17).

John C. Collins stated that "in prosperity, our friends know us; in adversity, we meet our friends." When Job's friends learned of his calamity, they went to him, in theory to console him (Job 2.11-13). From chapter 3, with a mistaken theology, Job's friends began to accuse him saying that his suffering was a reflection of his sins. Job was accused of being a liar, a Hypocrite, and guilty of the death of his children (Job 16:10). But even in the face of ridicule, contempt, and accusations, Job kept his integrity.

d) The Contempt of Bystanders.

From respected and honored to despised and mocked by society (Job 17:2). This was Job's situation when inserted in the distressing crisis (Job 29:7-11). Such was the desolation that Job felt like an animal of nocturnal habits that lived in the desert in solitude (Job 30:29). Job's calamity had become a matter of joy and play (Job 17:6; 30:9; Ps 69:12). The loss of prosperity entailed the loss of these honors.

The one who was flattered in wealth and success was cruelly despised in the time of adversity (Job 30:1-10). It is understood that Job's social life was affected when everything went wrong on the horizontal plane, that is, between men.

However, even desolate and in the midst of setbacks, on the vertical plane he remained faithful to the Lord, His God.

e) Faithful, even if the losses seem irreparable.

The speed and unpredictability of events in Job's life only show how transitory things are. The feast day turned into a day of mourning. We need to know how to face:

The Separation of The People We Love.

As painful as it is, death is a reality and, paradoxically, it is in the face of loss that our hearts tend to get better (Eccl 7:1-3). We will all have to live with this certainty until Jesus discontinues it, because in eternity with Christ there will be no more funeral processions or separations (Rev. 21:4).

It is worth keeping us faithful to God, even with our eyes tearing up for irreparable losses, because our crying cannot be the end of faith, nor the end of hope (I Thess. 4:13).

Jesus himself, faced with the momentary loss of Lazarus, although he knew he would resurrect him, could not contain himself and wept (John 11:35-44). Job was not the only one who faced the loss of the people he loved.

Many at this time may have their hearts torn by the gap left by someone who has gone, but, like Job, we must always remain faithful, because the one who gave life has the right to take it back (1Sm 2.6).

Loss of Material Goods

Faced with the reality of the loss of his possessions, Job clung to spiritual realities and therefore did not waver in his faith (Job 13:15). His faithfulness did not rest on what God does at this or that moment, but rested on what He is at all times.

Thus, the ephemerality of earthly properties, as well as the durability of spiritual realities are demonstrated throughout the book. Only a heart centered on God and His principles, such as Job's, can overcome all feelings of unbelief in unexpectedly unfavorable times (Job 2:21; Hc 3:17-19).

The Irrefutable Reality of Illnesses.

There is no denying that, because of sin, humanity is subject to all kinds of evils (Gen. 3:16-19). No one is free from being afflicted by diseases and infirmities (Rom. 3:23). However, it is in these situations that the true nature of faith is gauged (Job 2:4-6).

As if the fragile psychological state he was in wasn't enough, Job now saw his physical state being violently hit and his health slipping away (Job 2.7, 8).

It is in the context of anguish that the strength or weakness of the Christian will be revealed, whether he is faithful or unfaithful (Prov 24:10). Job, despite his pain and suffering, knew that God continued to watch and defend him (Job 16:19)

Even in the moments of greatest intensity of his pain, Job remained faithful (Job 2:10). The book of Job teaches us that diagnosis, irrefutable as it may seem, cannot contradict divine love and assistance (Ps. 46:1).

How to Stay Faithful Even in the Face of Life's Instabilities

It is not always easy to understand God's action, but discerning His Word and the conviction that God always wants the best for us will keep us stable in the face of life's vicissitudes.

f) Maintain Established Beliefs.

Although the word "faith" does not appear in the book of Job, it does appear in his life and behavior in face of the crisis that had taken place in his life (Heb. 11.1).

44

His convictions about God and His goodness were not shaken (Job 19:23). Job teaches us that where the wisdom of God manifests itself as unknown. The only way to be followed is that of faith (Heb 11:6). Thus, we learn that a man's theology will influence his life, for spiritual convictions are the roots of all others.

Whatever a man thinks about God and about his faith will mold his character and shape his destiny. Despite the sorrows, Job's faith anchored in God (Job 13:14-16).

Do not apply the Theology of Cause and Effect in Life.

It is understood from the Scriptures that suffering has sin as its primary cause.

However, not all suffering has sin as its immediate cause (Gen. 3:15-19); Jn 9:1-3). Cause-and-effect theology transfers fixity from the physical world to the spiritual world. For many, suffering is a reflection of the absence of God in life and, consequently, a hidden sin. This was the theological mindset of Eliphaz, Bildad, Zophar, and Elihu (Job 4.7, 8; 22.5). Job's faith was not shaken because he knew that tragedies can also befall those who know God.

Understand Divine Sovereignty.

Job does not attribute to the Devil the cause of his afflictions, as many do. The certainty of divine sovereignty gave her the serenity to worship Him in the day of perplexity (Job 1:20; Hc 3:17-18). He was aware that the divine will, which is sovereign, determines our coming and going in this short period of life (Job 1.21; Eccl 3.2).

There are not few who are inserted in adversity have difficulty reconciling goodness with the omnipotence of God. They ask: "If God is good and can do all things, why am I suffering?" C.S. Lewis, in his book "The Problem of Suffering", tells us how difficult, or even impossible.

Iit is to know with certainty what is good or bad in this life (Isa. 55:8, 9). The simultaneity of tragic events that happened in Job's life did not make him a bitter person. He was the victim of misunderstandings, suffered great losses and still did not lose kindness to others.

And he proved himself faithful to God (Job 42:10; 1.22). All that unleashing of afflictions that happened in his life served him as a test and improvement. Job came out of the crisis stronger, more lucid about God and about himself (Job 42:5,6). Even outside the boundaries of understanding and the brotherly love of relatives, friends and acquaintances, Job knew who he could count on: God." —SEARA'S PORTAL OF CHRIST. Loyalty in Times of Crisis, 2016

g) Have Hope

No other apostle called upon the church to remain hopeful in Christ than Paul, not only because he left us the greatest number of letters contained in the New

Testament, but because he even placed more emphasis on this dire need of the church. , of never losing the certainty that he is faithful and just to fulfill what he promised.

"This is a faithful word: that if we die with him, we will also live with him; if we suffer, we will also reign with him.

Se o negarmos, também ele nos negará; Se formos infiéis, ele permanece fiel; não pode negar-se a si mesmo. (2 Timóteo 2:11-13)" O apóstolo tinha a plena certeza de que nenhuma das promessas que o Senhor fez aos seus discípulos iriam falhar.

Por ser Deus, santo e justo sempre às cumprirá. "Deus não é homem, para que minta; nem filho do homem, para que se arrependa. Porventura diria ele, e não o faria? Ou falaria, e não o confirmaria?" (Números 23:19

The faithful god

"There is someone who is great in his loyalty. Faithfulness is a perfection in God whereby He is faithful to His Word and all His covenants. He never breaks a contract with himself or with his creatures. What He purposed it will do, and what He promised it will do. Lying is one of the most prevalent sins of all times.

It was believing a lie that ruined the entire human race. Adam and Eve left the Word of God and followed the father of lies. And all his children followed the same path. The children of Israel literally begged, in the distant past, the prophets to preach lies to them. They cried out:

"Do not prophesy to us what is right; tell us pleasant things, and see for us deceptions". Isaiah 30:10. In our days, the word lie is camouflaged with the term "propaganda". It is said that in Zion whoever was caught telling a lie would have his mouth sewn up for three days.

Brother RG Lee says, that if this were the law here in our country, many businessmen would not be able to answer the telephone, and that many ladies would walk around with beautiful embroidery in their mouths. The inclination to tell and believe a lie is one of the most startling facts in human history.

From the mouth of one Man, no lie ever came out. And this was the God-Man, Jesus Christ, truth incarnate. Isaiah 53:9.

God is true to himself

Of God we read that "If we are unfaithful, he remains faithful; he cannot deny himself". 2 Timothy 2:13. This means that He will accomplish all that He has purposed. Romans 8:28 says that everything works for the good of those who love God and are called according to his purpose. Back in eternity before, there was a people who once knew and predestined whom God purposed to call and justify and glorify.

This was a secret proposal, known only to God. There was no promise given to man, for man did not even exist yet. Therefore, if God did not call, justify and glorify the formerly known and predestined, He would neither be faithful nor true to Himself.

He would be like the man who set out to do one thing, and then failed through inconsistency or inability. God is faithful to his own purpose, and has ample power to carry out his plans. "And according to his will he works with the host of heaven and the inhabitants of the earth; there is no one who can hinder his hand, and say to him:

What are you doing"? Daniel 4:35.

God is faithful to his son — There are certain promises made to Christ, which is symbolized by David spiritually, on condition that he perform His duties as Mediator of the new covenant. And God had sworn not to lie to David, that is, to Christ, the spiritual David. He would see His seed and the labor of His soul and be satisfied.

In relation to the covenant of grace, of which the three persons of the Trinity were part, we cannot do better than to quote B. H. Carroll: "Before there was the world, a covenant of grace and mercy was made by the Father, Son, and Holy Spirit, whose evidences are full in the NT, and the part to be performed by each is clearly defined, viz.:

The grace of the Father in agreeing that his Son should come. **His obligations to the covenant of giving a seed to the Son, his foreknowledge of that seed, his predestination of the seed, and the justification and adoption of these in good time.**

Does the Son's covenant include the obligation to assume human nature in His incarnation, voluntarily renouncing the glory He had with the Father before the world? to become obedient even to death and death on the cross. The consideration as hope ahead of him, inducing him to bear the disgrace of the cross, and the reward given for obedience, was His resurrection, His glorification, His exaltation to the royal priestly throne, and His investment with right to judge.

And the obligations of the Holy Spirit were to apply his work of redemption in calling, convicting, regenerating, sanctifying, and raising up from the dead the seed promised to the Son. All of this shows that the plan of salvation was not an afterthought; that his roots in election and predestination are as much in eternity as in the existence of the world. And its fruits are in eternity after judgment. The believer must consider this chain, test every link, shake it and hear its sound, linked from eternity to eternity. Every one God has chosen is drawn by the Spirit to Christ. Every predestined one is called by the Spirit in time, justified in time, and will be glorified when the Lord comes."

Christ's death was not an experience

Christ's death was not an experience, uncertain of results. The work of the Holy Spirit is not a mere attempt to see how much He can do. We could never approve the doctrine of an unfaithful Father, a defeated Holy Spirit, and a disappointed Son. We believe in a faithful God, an invincible Holy Spirit and a victorious Christ. Spurgeon says:

"I firmly believe that every soul for whom Christ shed His blood as a substitute, He will claim as His, and rightfully His. I love this truth and delight in proclaiming it. Not all the powers of earth or hell, nor the stubbornness of the human will, nor the deep depravity of the human mind.

They can keep Christ from seeing his soul labor and being satisfied. John 6:13-40. But even better are the words uttered by the lips of Truth in the flesh… hear it: "All that the Father gives me will come to me; and what comes to me I will by no means cast away. Because I came down from heaven, not to do my will, but the will of the one who sent me. And the will of the Father who sent me is this: that none of all those who gave me may be lost, but that he may be raised on the last day". John 6:37-40

The foundation of our security

The basis of our security is the faithfulness of God to his Son. "God is faithful, by whom you were called into the fellowship of his Son Jesus Christ our Lord." 1 Corinthians 1:9.

According to the covenant, Jesus Christ would have companions. By God's call (the effectual call of the Spirit by the Word) we are first admitted into fellowship with Christ, and the ultimate goal is our presence with Him in glory. And this is guaranteed by God's faithfulness.

That will confirm us in the end (1 Corinthians 1:8), for the callings will be justified and glorified. Those He called and justified are safe as long as God is faithful to His Word to the Son.

Getting rid of correction depends on the believer's good conduct, but the assurance of glory is based on God's faithfulness to His Son. "If your children forsake my law, and walk not in my judgments, if they profane my precepts, and keep my commandments, then I will visit with a rod, and their iniquity with stripes.

But I will not totally withdraw my kindness from him, nor will I fail in my faithfulness. I won't break my alliance; I won't alter what came out of my lips. I once swore on my holiness that I would not lie to David. His seed will last forever, and his throne will be like the sun before me". Psalm 89:30-36. What a firm foundation for our faith! Our security does not lie in our faithfulness to God, but in God's faithfulness to his Son. ALELUIA1

God Is Faithful To His Saints

God made promises to the poor, weak, and saddened believers who believed in the Lord Jesus Christ and He will faithfully fulfill every promise he made. "For the gifts and calling of God are without repentance." Romans 11:29. This means that God is faithful to His covenant promises, and will not fail to glorify those He has called. All of God's promises in Christ are "yes" (sure) so that every believer can say "amen" to the glory of God. 2 Corinthians 1:20.

Preservation

God is faithful in preserving His people. "Because the Lord loves judgment and does not forsake his saints, they are preserved forever."

Psalm 37:28. "My sheep hear my voice, and I know them, and they follow me; and I give them eternal life, and they shall never perish.

And no one will snatch them from my hand. My Father, who, but gave, is greater than all; and no one can snatch them out of my Father's hand." John 10:27-29. He who is preserved does not have the power to guard himself. The saints are weak, but they are kept by the power of God.

1 Peter 1:5. God's promise to the believer is eternal life. And this does not mean eternal existence, but eternal favor or justification so that he is never again under condemnation. John 5:24.

"And the God of peace himself sanctify you in all things; and all your spirit, and soul, and body, be fully kept blameless for the coming of our Lord Jesus Christ. Faithful is what calls you, who will also do it". 1 Thessalonians 5:23-24. Here lies complete sanctification and deliverance from sin and this by the believer's dependence on God's faithfulness.

Calls are not only justified but also glorified, for God is faithful. God would never call sinners with the effectual call of eternal life and then leave them halfway to glory. God's work for His saints is perfect.

Those who have fled the storm of divine wrath, have the Word of God, and His oath as a basis of hope, these two things being immutable, in which God cannot lie. Discipline - God is faithful in disciplining His children. "I know, O Lord, that your judgments are just.

And according to your faithfulness you afflicted me". Psalm 119:75. Here David submits to God's discipline and accepts it as just and good. In David's theology there was no place for luck or chance.

He believed that whatever happened was ordained by God. His afflictions were great, but he saw the hand of God in all of them, and he believed they were for his own good. He further adds that God was faithful to send them.

God was working for David's well, and he knew what he needed. God is as faithful to his in disciplining them as he is in preserving them. God is not an indulgent and unfaithful Eli.

He will not allow His children to sin without being disciplined. "He who does not use the rod hates his son, but the one who loves him punishes him from an early age." Proverbs 13:24. We should praise God for His faithfulness in lashing us in order to bring us back to Himself.

And to the paths of obedience. The saints have certain tendencies of the sheep and are prone to go astray. God is the faithful shepherd who knows how to use the rod to bring us back to the flock. Listen to David again:

"Before I was afflicted, I went wrong; but now I have kept your word". Psalm 119:67. And the doctrine remains the same, whether in the Old or New Testament. In Hebrews 12:11 we read:

"And, in fact, every correction, at present, does not seem to be of joy, but of sadness, but later produces a peaceful fruit of justice in those exercised by it." We have this glorious truth written by one of the Puritans, Thomas Washburn (1606-1687):

As the saint grows in the wisdom of truth concerning God and man, he will disown himself and admire God more and more. When the truth about God and the individual sinks in, then we will do what is right, we will love mercy, and we will walk in humility before God. Micah 6:8.

O how much we, his blood-bought children, must be faithful to him who will never fail in faithfulness to us! This is what He requires of us as stewards of His goods. It will matter little when we die, if we have riches and honors in this world, but it will matter greatly if we are faithful to our Redeemer.

May the faithfulness of God produce in us fountains from which flow waters of faithfulness in his glorious service. — *PRUDENT WORD. Bible, Definition of Doctrine, volume-1, chapter 17 God's Faithfulness, 2015*

Therefore, because we are sure, through the Scriptures, of the faithfulness of this God who gave the life of his only Son to rescue us from our trespasses and sins, we must live in complete peace of mind, knowing that none of his promises will fail.

In due time they will be fulfilled and the victory of the church is already certain. Let us look at the trajectory she has taken in the course of these more than two thousand years, all the persecution she has suffered and the punishment thousands of Christians have been subjected to. And yet, the chosen one of the Lord remained standing, firm in the face of so many trials.

Enduring all sorts of affronts and sneers, to be prepared for your big day at the end. Let us never forget that it is not enough just to have faith, it is necessary to have works of righteousness, because faith without attitude is dead (James 2:26) And the main attitude to be taken is to remain faithful, sanctified.

Believers that our efforts to abandon our worldly ways to await the Lord's coming is not in vain. "Jesus promised His disciples that He would return again. The Bible says in John 14:1-3 "Do not let your hearts be troubled; believe in God, believe also in me.

In my father's house there are many abodes; otherwise, I would have told you; I will prepare a place for you. And if I go and prepare a place for you, I will come again, and I will take you to myself, that wherever I am you may be also."

"The angels promised that Jesus would come again. The Bible says in Acts 1:10-11 "While their eyes were fixed on heaven as he was going up, behold.

Two men dressed in white appeared by them, and they said to them, 'Galilean men, why do you stand there looking at the sky? This Jesus, who was taken up from among you into heaven, will come as you saw him go into heaven."

How will Jesus' return? The Bible says in Luke 21:27 "Then shall they see the son of man coming in a cloud with power and great glory." How many will see Him when He comes?

The Bible says in Revelation 1:7 "Behold, he cometh with clouds, and every eye shall see him, even those who pierced him; and all the tribes of the earth will mourn over him. Yes, Amen.

"What will we see and hear when He returns? The Bible says in 1 Thessalonians 4:16-17 "For the Lord Himself will descend from heaven with a loud cry, at the voice of the archangel, at the sound of the trumpet of God, and those who died in Christ shall rise first.

Then we who are left alive will be caught up with them in the clouds to meet the Lord in the air, and thus we will be with the Lord forever. "How visible will his Coming be? The Bible says in Matthew 24:27 "For as the lightning goes out from the east and shines to the west, so shall the coming of the son of man be"

How did Jesus prevent us from being deceived about his Second Coming? The Bible says in Matthew 24:23-26 "If than anyone should say to you, here is the Christ! or: Hey there! believe not; for false chorists and false prophets shall arise, and shall do great signs and wonders; so that, if possible, they would deceive even the chosen ones. Behold, I have told you beforehand.

Therefore, if they say unto you, Behold, he is in the wilderness; do not go out; or: Behold, he is inside the house; do not believe." Does anyone know the exact time of his coming? The Bible says in Matthew 24:36 "But no one knows of that

Day and hour, not the angels of heaven. not the son, but only the father." Knowing how human it is to put off everything, what does Christ tell us to do? The Bible says in Matthew 24:42 "Watch therefore, for ye know not what day your Lord cometh." How did Jesus prevent us from being surprised by this event? We read in Luke 21:34-36: "Look after yourselves; lest your hearts be burdened with gluttony, drunkenness, and the cares of life, and that day should come upon you suddenly like a snare. For it will come upon all that dwell on the face of the earth.

Watch therefore at all times, praying, that you may escape from all these things that are to come, and stand in the presence of the Son of man". Why is Jesus taking so long? The Bible says in 2 Peter 3:8-9 "But you, beloved ones, do not ignore one thing: that one day with the Lord is like a thousand years, and a thousand years like one day.

The Lord does not delay his promise, though some regard it as late; but he is long-suffering with you, not wanting anyone to be lost, but everyone to come to repent." While we wait for Jesus, how should we live our life? The Bible says in Titus 2:11-14 "For the grace of God was manifested, bringing salvation to all men, teaching us, that, forsaking ungodliness and worldly passions, we might live in the present sober and righteous world, and piously.

Looking forward to the blessed hope and glorious appearing of our great God and Savior Jesus Christ. Who gave himself for us to redeem us from all iniquity, and to purify for himself a people all of him, zealous of good works"? How will the world be when Jesus returns? The Bible says in Matthew 24:37-39 "For as it was said in the days of Noah, so will the coming of the Son of man be also. For, just as in the days before the flood, they ate, drank, married, and gave in marriage. Until the day that Noah entered the ark, and they did not realize it, until the flood came, and took them all away; so, shall the coming of the Son of man be also."

Will the Coming of Christ be a time for rewards? The Bible says in Matthew 16:27 "For the Son of man will come in the glory of his Father, with his angels; and then he will repay each according to his works." The Bible says in Revelation 22:12: "He that is unjust, let him still do unrighteousness: and he that is dirty, let him still be soiled; and whoever is just, do justice still; and whoever is holy, sanctify himself still." Why will Jesus' return?

The Bible says in Hebrews 9:28 "So Christ, offering himself once to bear the sins of many, will appear a second time, without sin, to those who wait for him for salvation." At Christ's Second Coming, we will finally have the complete reality of our salvation.

The Bible says in 1 Corinthians 1:7-8 "Therefore you lack no gift, while you wait for the manifestation of our Lord Jesus Christ, who will also confirm you to the end, that you may be blameless in the day of our Lord Jesus Christ." — *BIBLEINFO.COM PORTAL. The Second Coming of Jesus, 2012*

The foundation that structures the foundation of the Christian faith is the promise that soon Jesus will return to take his church, this guarantee given to us by himself in the gospels.

Peter emphasized the Christians of his time, and of all times to come, to remain alert to this important day and not tire of waiting for it, as unbelievers do, wondering when it will happen, for God is in no hurry.

In satisfying man's expectations, but the return of Christ will be in the day established by him, when he sees fit for it to happen.

However, the apostle explains that it will happen by surprise, at a time when the world will not be waiting, "in the blink of an eye." Humanity lives in times of deep apostasy, where faith in God and His promises have been forgotten.

And most Christians are getting carried away by this unbelief regarding the coming of the Lord, claiming to be too long.

In this, Peter warned us not to be ignorant:

"Beloved ones, I now write to you this second letter, in both of which I arouse your sincere spirit with exhortation. That you may remember the words that were first spoken by the holy prophets, and our commandment, as apostles of the Lord and Savior. Knowing this first, that in the last days there will come scoffers, walking after their own lusts, and saying, where is the promise of his coming? Because since the parents slept, all things remain the same since the beginning of creation?

They voluntarily ignore this, that by the word of God the heavens existed from ancient times, and the earth, which was taken out of the water and in the midst of the water, subsists. By which things perished the world then, covered with the waters of the flood. But the heavens and the earth which are now by the same word are kept for a treasure, and are kept for fire, until the day of judgment, and the perdition of ungodly men.

But, beloved ones, do not ignore one thing, that one day with the Lord is like a thousand years, and a thousand years like one day. The Lord does not delay his promise, though some regard it as late; but he is long-suffering with us, not wanting some to be lost.

But all to come to repent. But the day of the Lord will come like a thief in the night; in which the heavens will pass away with a great noise, and the elements, burning, will melt away, and the earth, and the works that are in it, will be burned.

Wherefore all these things must perish, what persons it is fitting for you to be in holy dealing, and godliness, Waiting and hastening for the coming of the day of God, in which the heavens shall melt with fire, and the elements.

Burning, will they merge? But we, according to his promise, await new heavens and a new earth, in which righteousness dwells. Therefore, beloved, awaiting these things, seek that from him you may be found immaculate and blameless in peace. And count the longsuffering of our Lord for salvation. As also our beloved brother Paul wrote to you, according to the wisdom given him; speaking of this, as in all his epistles, among which there are points difficult to understand, which the unlearned and fickle twist.

And so are the other Scriptures, to their own perdition. Therefore, beloved ye, knowing this beforehand, beware that by the deception of abominable men ye may be caught up together, and fall from your steadfastness; rather grow in the grace and knowledge of our Lord and Savior, Jesus Christ. To him be the glory, so now, as in the day of eternity. Amen". (2 Peter 3:1-18)

If the church fails to believe in Christ's return and His rapture, remaining faithful will become useless. And that's why Satan insists on leading modern man into this absurd disbelief, giving the idea that Jesus has only deceived his disciples with such a promise. In this case, what is evident from this insinuation is that the Lord is a liar. that, to keep himself alive in the memory of those who believed in his teachings, he planted in their minds this mad hope.

For the enemies of God, the Son he died on the cross and never rose again, and with him all his teachings also died. But for us, the truly chosen ones and heirs of divine grace, our Savior is alive and seated at the right hand of the Father Almighty, reigning over heaven and earth, preparing to return and take us to dwell with him in heavenly mansions. Paul, too, mentions the day of the rapture to the Thessalonian brothers. And, in Peter's likeness, he urges caution in preserving hope regarding Christ's second coming to this world, this time in glory and power, in order to rescue his chosen ones.

He warns the church to keep alert and sanctified lest it be surprised by this event. The reason for this awakening is because among Christians there are always the fickle ones. Who slumber in vigilance, neither pray nor seek to be constantly in the presence of the Lord?

And, these, end up getting too involved with secular things, participating in the delicacies offered by the Devil and contaminating themselves with the delicacies of this world alienated from God.

And today, more than ever, the church needs to be reminded of these counsels left by the apostles of Christ to all generations. It is imperative that modern preachers begin again to remind Christians that the coming of our Savior is near and the time has come for us to be prepared.

"But, brothers, concerning times and seasons, you do not need to be written to. For you yourselves know very well that the day of the Lord will come like a thief in the night. For when they say:

There is peace and security, then sudden destruction will come upon them, like the birth pangs of one who is pregnant, and they will by no means escape. But you, brothers, are no longer in darkness, so that that day may overtake you like a thief.

For you are all children of the light and children of the day; we are neither of the night nor of the darkness. Let us not sleep, then, like the rest, but let us watch, and let us be sober. For those who sleep, sleep at night, and those who get drunk, get drunk at night.

But we who are of the day, let us be sober, putting on the breastplate of faith and love, and having the hope of salvation for our helmet. For God has not destined us for wrath, but for the purchase of salvation, through our Lord Jesus Christ, who died for us, that, whether we watch or sleep, we may live in union with Him.

Therefore comfort one another and build one another up, even as you are doing" (1 Thessalonians 5:1-11) Hope in God, therefore, must be constant in our lives. Nothing, not even the worst of afflictions, should keep us from continuing to wait on him with faith and hope. Of course, the Lord's church will always face incomparable struggles and trials during its journey on earth. Now, for sure, different from what happened before.

Because, contrary to past centuries, we conquered religious freedom in all Western countries, even if in the East there is still resistance from countries dominated by Islam. And, with all this freedom that we have, especially in Brazil, where everyone chooses who to believe and worship, it was immensely easy to serve God. In fact, so easy that most Christians get corrupted and turn the Gospel into a way to generate income, religion is transformed day by day into a way to earn money by selling blessings and miracles.

In the name of Jesus. But despite the growing tide of false prophets and lost workers that plague our pulpits, none of this undoes the promise made regarding the Lord's return and the rapture of his Bride. God never tires of alerting all his chosen ones, through his Word preached to the four corners of the world. From the manifestations of his Spirit, from the fulfillment of his prophecies announced in the revelation of the Apocalypse. So that they don't get tired of waiting for the return of their Son at any moment to take them to him, suddenly, like lightning, when least expected.

The end comes, of that we are absolutely sure. Just like in Noah's time, where he preached the flood and all his contemporaries who ate and drank. they peacefully lived their dissolute lives without caring for the warnings of the servant of God, until the flood waters came and destroyed every living thing in the ancient world, with the exception of Noah and his family (Luke 17:27)

The Resurrection of the Dead (1 Theses 4. 16)

"For the Lord Himself will descend from heaven with a shout, and with the voice of an archangel, and with the trumpet of God; and those who died in Christ will rise first". Moments before the rapture, when Christ descends from heaven to seek his church, there will be the resurrection of the dead, those who died in Christ.

Living Believers Will Be Transformed

Living believers will be transformed; their bodies will clothe themselves with immortality. The apostle Paul says in 1 Corinthians 15. 51, 52 "Behold, I tell you a mystery: we will not all sleep, but we will all be transformed, in a moment, in the twinkling of an eye, at the sound of the last trumpet. The trumpet will sound, the dead will rise incorruptible, and we will be changed."

Although Jesus did not come during Paul's lifetime, he was hopeful that Jesus would come back even then, and he preached that Jesus would come back at any time. Believers today must have that same hope, we are in the last minute, we must live in the hope that Jesus will come back during our lifetime, he will come back today!

We Will Meet with Christ in The Air (1 Theses 4. 17)

We will meet the Lord in the clouds, in the air and thus we will be with Him forever. We will be literally united with Christ, taken to the Father's house in heaven, in John 14. 2, 3 tells us: "In my father's house to many addresses, if not so, I would have already told you.

Well, I'm going to prepare a place for you. And when I go and prepare a place for you, I will return and receive you to myself, that, where I am, you may also be." When we get there, we will join the dear ones who had died, in 1 This 4. 13, 14 the apostle Paul tells us: "I don't want you to be ignorant of those who are already asleep, so that you won't be sad...

Because if we believe that Jesus died and rose again so also those who died in Jesus God will again bring them with Him." When the rapture of the church takes place, we will be free from all afflictions, all persecutions, all oppression, all dominion of sin and death, the rapture will deliver us from the "future wrath", that is, from the great tribulation.

The bible insists that we yearn and that we continually and confidently wait for the return of our Lord. Romans 13, 11 tells us that our salvation is now, closer than when we first believed. In Revelation 22: 12, 20 tells us: "And, behold, I come without delay, and with me is the reward that I have to repay each one according to her works.

He who bears witness to these things says: Surely, I come without delay. Amen! Come Lord Jesus! — *ANDRADE, MÁRCIO. Portal Gospel Mays, The Rapture of the Church, 2012*

There are several studies, sermons, biblical commentaries, published Books and speeches made by the most renowned scholars of the Holy Scriptures regarding the second coming of Jesus Christ to this world, on the need for all Christians to remain believers in this divine promise that, with all sure, it will not fail to be fulfilled. All the suffering of the ancient Christians, who gave their lives to fire, the sword, the rude cross and the dungeons, as well as the most terrible tortures.

And it was because they faithfully believed in the promises that they would dwell with their God in heavenly mansions. And this must also be our eternal hope. This victory is already reserved for those who remain firm in the trust they once embraced, for those who do not back down or deny the name of the one who gave his life so that, through such a sublime sacrifice, we might be saved. So, let's move on, with our heads held high and convinced that he will soon return.

3 - THE TRUE CHURCH

When we speak of "church" we are not referring to the temple plaque, bearing the name of this or that particular religion, but rather the one that was born in Jerusalem with Christ and his apostles, and which continued through each new convert from the first Christian century to today. In fact, there are three distinct spiritual phases of the true church that can be characterized as ideological or philosophical cycles of the Christian faith.

These cycles are the varied ways in which man began to interpret the Holy Scriptures. Under the prism of doubts and inquiries. Unlike first century Christians, when the belief in what was sacred and divine was the basis of everything, after human beings started to look down and value earthly things, much was lost from the spiritual values acquired in the foundations of the Christian faith.

1 First Phase — The True Church — The first spiritual cycle of the church of Christ, considered the most important for being the one where faith in everything that was taught by its founder. The Messiah, was solid and without a shadow of doubts and questions on the part of those who had been converted to the Gospel. This phase is called the Primitive Church, the most perfect and faithful to divine principles. Among those Christians indeed existed the essence of true love, the most living faith in God, and the constant presence of the Holy Spirit in the lives of all the saved. At no other time in the Christian church has such spiritual purity and such devotion to the teachings left by Jesus Christ been seen. There was no room for envy, ambition. Love of money or for the material riches of this world or for the unbridled passions of this world that cause so much scandal and shame the name of God in our day.

Despite the tremendous persecutions by those who oppose the cross of Christ and the Good News message, they persevered. Thus relates Luke in his account sent to Theophilus, in the book of "The Acts of the Apostles": "And the heart and soul of the multitude of those who believed was one, and none said that anything he possessed was his own, but all things were common to them.

And the apostles bore, with great power, testimony of the resurrection of the Lord Jesus, and in all of them there was abundant grace. There was, therefore, none among them in need; for all who owned estates or houses, selling them, brought the price of what had been sold, and laid it at the feet of the apostles. And it was distributed to each one, according to the needs that each one had." Acts 4:32-35

Faith based on the teachings of Christ, sanctity of soul and body, moral character, integrity in everything he said and did, complete devotion to Christianity, doctrine learned from the apostles, Christian sincerity, unity and the detachment from material goods to the point of not seeing those who refused to share what they had with those who had nothing. These were the most striking characteristics of the church born in the first century of the Christian Era, right after the death and resurrection of the Lord. This stage of the church was where the most important facts of the New Testament took place, such as:

The witness and death of the early Christians under various persecutions of the professing opposers of the new faith, the conversion of Saul, the persecutor of the faithful, who then he assumed the pseudonym of Paul and became the most important defender and expander of the Gospel among Gentiles. Non-Jewish peoples, through the first missionary journeys. In it occurred the arrest and death of the apostles, the exile of John on the Isle of Patmos. Where he received from the Lord the revelation of the Apocalypse and the end of time. Many Christians were beheaded, burned and buried alive.

Others eaten by wild beasts in public shows at the Coliseum in Rome. Before the emperor and those who applauded such carnage, but did not deny their faith. The writer of the letter to the Hebrews reports this time and the glory achieved by the valiant Christians: "Who by faith conquered kingdoms, practiced righteousness, obtained promises, shut the mouths of the lions.

They quenched the strength of the fire, escaped the edge of the sword, drew strength from weakness, struggled in battle, put to fight the armies of strangers. Women received their dead by resurrection. Some were tortured, not accepting their release, to achieve a better resurrection, and others experienced mocking and whipping, and even jails and prisons. They were stoned, sawed, tempted, slain at the edge of the sword; they walked in the skins of sheep and goats, helpless, afflicted and abused (Of which the world was not worthy), wandering in the deserts, and in the mountains, and in the pits and caves of the earth." Hebrews 11:33-38

Comparing the spiritual quality of the early church with that of today, we can easily see the enormous antagonism between it and the current one, today it has become difficult, or why not to say almost impossible, to identify true Christians who can be seen as authentic representatives of Christ in this world.

The church of the first century, which was pure, holy and true, became a mere factory of charlatans, specialized in deceiving the people and selling the miracles given by the Holy Spirit. Without a doubt there was no period before when the name of the Most High was more muddied by religious corruption than it is now. Certainly, the church reformers and those who bloodily defended religious freedom from the Great Protestant Reformation. Started in the 14th century by Luther, who sought to allow everyone the right to have access to the Holy Scriptures until then locked under lock and key in Rome. They would be ashamed of what the result of all their efforts has become.

However, the first phase of the Christian church still shines through in the history and memory of those who truly converted to Christianity and actually gave their lives to the Lord Jesus. And it is taken as an example by all Christians who still remain faithful despite the cloud of darkness in the form of corruption and shame. In which modern religions are almost totally involved. We will never again experience an almost spiritually perfect period in terms of faith and holiness, but we can continue to believe and hope in the promises of the Savior.

Characteristics of the True Church

"Where can the true church be found today and what are its essential aspects? In the first place we must distinguish the various meanings of the word church:

1. All the people of God in all ages, the total ensemble of the elect. The Reformers spoke of this as the invisible church.

2. The local community of Christians, visibly gathered for worship and ministry; this meaning encompasses the vast majority of New Testament references to the church (ekklesia).

3. All of God's people in the world, at any one time, perhaps best defined as the universal church. This sense occurs only occasionally in the New Testament (1 Corinthians 10:32; Galatians 1:13).

4. "The church within the church." We noted rather the distinction made between the edah (the entire visible congregation)

And the gahal (those within it who respond to God's call). Jesus taught that the kingdom corresponds to this pattern: tares are mixed with wheat (Matthew 13:24-30; 36-43). Within the group identified with Christ are found the people of God, the true church. There is, then, no pure church; among every church there may be people who have not professed their faith.

68

And others whose profession will be unmasked at the last day (Matthew 7:21-23). Assuming thus that a pure or perfect church is not possible on this side of glory, where can we discover the true people of God visibly gathered together? Traditionally, four signs of the authentic church are recognized. ONE — The unity of the church proceeds from its foundation of the one God (Ephesians 4:1-6). All who truly belong to the church are one people, and therefore the true church will be distinguished by its unity. This unity, however, does not necessarily imply total uniformity.

In the New Testament church there was a variety of ministries (1 Corinthians 12:4-6) and opinions on matters of secondary importance (Romans 14:1-15:13). Although there was uniformity in basic theological convictions (1 Corinthians 15:11, BLH; Jude 3)

The common faith received different emphasis, according to the different needs perceived by the apostles. There were also a variety of forms of worship. The type of worship in Corinth (1 Corinthians 14.26ff) was not common in Palestinian churches, where worship was based on the Jewish synagogue model and had a more formal pattern centered on exposition of the written word.

This model taken from the synagogue justifies the fact that the first century churches were considered a branch of Judaism. James 2:2 even uses the word synagogue for the gathering of Christians. There are also discernible elements of more than one form of church government. The true unity in the Holy Spirit of all regenerate people is a fact independent of outward denominational disunity. The call to unity in the New Testament is therefore a command to maintain the fundamental oneness of life that the Spirit has bestowed through regeneration (Ephesians 4:3). The Reformers stressed this point, distinguishing between the invisible church.

(All the elect who are truly one in Christ) and the visible church (a mixed group of regenerate and unregenerate). The unity of the invisible church is a fait accompli, given with salvation. Rome has used this sign controversially in order to proclaim its unity, comparing it to the fragmentation of Protestantism.

As an evidence of being the true church. This, however, ignores three points: (i) Rome itself split from the Orthodox Church in 1054, and had never been universally regarded as the only true church in previous centuries. For example, the Celtic church flourished in England, and Patrick founded the English church long before Roman missionaries reached England. (ii) Signs must stick together.

Historical succession and outward unity have no validity when not associated with loyalty and the apostolic gospel. Although Protestantism has sometimes proved necessarily disruptive, it can be argued that, through its deviation from biblical doctrine, it is Rome itself that has been the greatest cause of schisms over the centuries.

The Scriptures encourage the fullest possible expression of unity among God's people, but they also make it clear that division is perfectly in keeping with the divine will when the essence of Apostolic Christianity is at stake.

This was the reason for the discord between Paul and the Judaizers (Galatians 1.6-12) And between Jesus and the Pharisees (Mark 7:1-13). It is significant to note that when Judas intended to write about the salvation we have in common.

He found it necessary to urge readers to "conflict diligently for the faith that was once delivered to the saints" (Jude 3). For the New Testament, unity is based on a conscious commitment. With the revealed truths of Apostolic Christianity.

The New Testament directed its teachings on unity to specific groups. With immediate implications for your visible relationships (Ephesians 2.15; 4.4; Col 3.15).

Jesus prayed for unity, which would help the world to believe (John 17:21); although the parallel between this unity and his with the Father (17.11,22) Confirming the essentially spiritual character of biblical unity, it certainly includes visible identification of life and purpose.

Por Jesus throughout his mission expressed a visible and demonstrable union with the father. one that is being experienced by those who are faithful to the apostolic gospel. This fact is especially important when two or more groups that have a biblical faith are operating in the same area, for example, on a university campus. The deepest challenge of this teaching, however, is at the level of relationships in the local church. In such an environment, the unity of life in Christ must be expressed through genuine and tangible care and commitment to one another. In the absence of this, the claim to be a true Christian church is called into question (1 Cor 3.3ff).

HOLY — God's people form the holy nation (1 Peter 2:9). In the deepest sense the church is holy. Just as every individual Christian is holy by virtue of being united with Christ, set apart for him, and clothed in his perfect righteousness. In its position before God in Christ, the church is blameless and free from any moral stain. The distinction between the visible and the invisible church applies here.

Since this imputed holiness does not belong to church members who do not personally trust Christ as Savior. Union with Christ also involves a holiness of life that is visible. Thus, the church's relationship with Christ. Your head will be expressed in the moral character and special characteristics of your life and community relationships. The church alien to holiness is alien to Christ. When Christ addressed his church, he expected this same moral difference from her and was stern in his judgment when he noted what they lacked (Revelation 2: -3). Lest we be discouraged when applying this test.

It is worth remembering that much of the life of the New Testament church was riddled with errors, divisions, moral flaws, and instability. Nevertheless, the presence of a visible sign of holiness is an invariable characteristic of God's church.

CATHOLIC (universal) — The term Catholic literally means embracing the whole. And in its early usage, it meant to be the universal church, distinguishing it from the local. It later came to mean the church that professed the orthodox faith, in contrast to the heretics. Over time, Rome adopted the term to refer to itself as an ecclesiastical institution, centered on the papacy, historically developed, and geographically widespread.

The sixteenth-century reformers sought to restore the former meaning of catholicity, in terms of the recognition of the orthodox faith; in that sense, they argued, the Catholic Church was in fact they and not Rome. The main aspect of the early church's catholicity was its openness to everyone. Distinct from Judaism, with its racial exclusivism, and from Gnosticism, with its cultural and intellectual exclusivism. The church opened its arms to everyone who wanted to hear the message and accept their savior. Without taking into account color, race, social status, intellectual capacity and moral background. It appeared in the world as a faith for all (Matthew 28:19; Revelation 7:9).

The only requirement for admission was personal faith in Jesus Christ as Savior and Lord. With baptism as the authorized rite of entry, because it manifested the gospel of grace (Matthew 28:19; Acts 2:38,41). It is at this fundamental level that this characteristic (that of being Catholic) must be understood. Churches that require further testing should be considered suspicious. There is no place in a true church for discrimination of any kind, whether racial, color or social. Intellectual or moral, in the latter case provided there is evidence of true repentance. Denominational discrimination also needs to be carefully examined in cases where...

The Church Through the Ages

Fundamental biblical doctrines are clearly recognized. **APOSTOLIC** — The apostle is a witness to the ministry and resurrection of Jesus; he is an authorized herald of the gospel (Luke 6:12ff; Acts 1:21ff; 1Cor 15:8-10). Heralds take their stand between Jesus and all subsequent generations of the Christian faith; we only come to him through the apostles and their testimony about him, embodied in the New Testament. In this fundamental sense, the entire church is "built on the foundation of the apostles" (Ephesians 2:20; see. Matthew 16:18; Revelation 21:14).

The apostolic power of the church therefore lies in the fact that it conforms to the apostolic faith "which was once and for all given to the saints." (Jude 3; cf. Acts 2:42). The apostles still govern and organize the church insofar as it allows its life, understanding and preaching to be constantly reformed by the teachings of the Holy Scriptures. Since apostle literally means sent, it is not surprising that the New Testament occasionally refers to other apostles (Romans 16:7). In this general sense, all those who are sent by the Lord today as evangelists, preachers, church starters, etc. they are in the New Testament Greek, apostles, sent.

This does not suggest a church perfectly fitting into this historical succession that needed the sixteenth-century Reformation, not to mention other minor reformations like the eighteenth-century awakening with Whitefield and the Wesley's. Roman Catholicism extends this interpretation of "apostolic" to include the claim that the Bishop of Rome is the historical successor of Peter and the special guardian of God's grace in the church.

The claim is untenable. Peter's primacy among the apostles was nothing more than a clear leadership in the period of the first Christian mission. He clearly retreated into the background as the church advanced out of Jerusalem, with Paul being appointed to lead the mission outside Palestine.

73

And as John struggled to correct churches harmed by false teachers. It is quite significant that Peter did not appear in the lead role at the Jerusalem Council (Acts 15). And that he clearly stood in the shadow of Paul in the incident recorded in Galatians 2. Rome further claims that this supposed supremacy of Peter should continue for the eternal and continuing salvation of the church. None of the verses cited as scriptural support (Matthew 16:18ff; John 21:15-17 and Luke 22:32) make any reference to a successor to Peter.

These two Roman claims contradict the evidence manifest in the New Testament, and the third, that Peter's primacy extends to the bishop of Rome, is even less credible. That Peter ended his life as a martyr in Rome is a primitive tradition. Who finds reasonable support; the historical difficulties, however, in showing that there was an established succession of monarchic bishops of Rome from the first century onwards, are insurmountable? Apostolic succession is actually the succession of the apostolic gospel. When the original deposit of apostolic truth is passed down from one generation to another: "faithful men…To instruct others" (2 Timothy 2:2).

The church is apostolic insofar as it recognizes in practice the supreme authority of the Apostolic Scriptures" — *FIC SERVIÇOS EDUCACIONAIS LTDA. Undergraduate Open Course*

The Origin of Christianity

Christianity is one of the so-called great religions. It has approximately 2 billion followers worldwide, including Catholics, Orthodox and Protestants. Christianity comes from the word Christ, which means messiah, consecrated person, anointed.

From the Hebrew mashiah (the savior) was translated into Greek as khristos and into Latin as christus.

The doctrine of Christianity is based on the belief that every human being is eternal, like Christ, who rose after his death. The Christian faith teaches that the present life is a journey and that death is a passage to an eternal and happy life for all who follow the teachings of Christ.

The teachings are contained exclusively in the Bible, divided between the Old and New Testaments. The Old Testament deals with the Jewish law, or Torah. It begins with accounts of creation and is all permeated by the promise that God, revealed to Abraham, Moses, and the prophets, would send his own son to earth as the Messiah. the Savior.

The New Testament contains the teachings of Christ, written by his followers. The main ones are the four gospels ("message", "good news"), written by the apostles Matthew, Mark, Luke and John. It also includes the Acts of the Apostles (letters and teachings that were passed on by word of mouth in the early Christian era, with emphasis on Paul's letters) and the Apocalypse. The birth of Christianity is intertwined with the history of the Roman Empire and the history of the Jewish people. At its origin, Christianity was touted as a sect arising out of Judaism and terribly persecuted. When Jesus Christ was born, around the year 4 BC, in the small city of Bethlehem, near Jerusalem, the Romans dominated Palestine.

The Jews lived under the administration of Roman governors and, therefore, aspired for the arrival of the Messiah (they believed that he would be a great man of war and that he would rule politically) Appointed in the Torah (VT) as the envoy who would free them from Roman domination Until the age of 30, Jesus lived anonymously in Nazareth, a city located in the north of present-day Israel. At age 33 he would be crucified in Jerusalem and resurrect three days later. In a short time, approximately three years, he gathered followers (the 12 apostles) and toured the region preaching his doctrine and performing miracles.

How to raise dead people and heal the blind, he soon became known to all and large crowds followed him. But to the Jewish religious authorities he was a blasphemer, as he called himself the Messiah. He lacked the looks and power to be the leader who would free the region from Roman domination.

He just preached peace, love of neighbor. To the Romans he was a popular agitator. After being arrested and killed, the tendency was for his followers to disperse. And his teachings were forgotten.

The opposite happened. It is precisely on this fact that the Christian faith is based. As the prophets in the Old Testament had anticipated, Christ rose, appeared to his apostles (Apostle means sent.)

Who were hidden and ordered them to spread throughout the world preaching his message of love, peace, restoration and salvation? Christianity established itself as a religion of divine origin. Its founder was the very son of God.

Sent as savior and builder of history together with man. To be a Christian, therefore, would be to engage in Christ's redemptive work, based on faith in his teachings. Quickly, Christian doctrine spread throughout the Mediterranean region and reached the heart of the Roman Empire.

The spread of Christianity throughout Greece and Asia Minor was the work of the apostle Paul, who was not one of the 12 and would have been called to the mission by Jesus himself. Christian communities multiplied. Rivalries arose and in Rome, many Christians were turned into martyrs.

Eaten by lions at Colosseum shows, as targets of the wrath of emperors beset by corruption and debauchery. Christianity is one of the so-called great religions. It has approximately 2 billion followers worldwide, including Catholics, Orthodox and Protestants.

Christianity comes from the word Christ, which means messiah, consecrated person, anointed. From the Hebrew mashiah (the savior) was translated into Greek as khristos and into Latin as christus. The doctrine of Christianity is based on the belief that every human being is eternal, like Christ, who rose after his death. The Christian faith teaches that the present life is a journey.

And that death is a passage to an eternal and happy life for all who follow the teachings of Christ the teachings are contained exclusively in the Bible, divided between the Old and New Testaments.

The Old Testament deals with the Jewish law, or Torah. It starts with accounts of creation and is all permeated by the promise that God. Revealed to Abraham, Moses, and the prophets, he would send his own son to earth as Messiah, the savior.

The New Testament contains the teachings of Christ, written by his followers. The main ones are the four gospels ("message", "good news"). Written by the apostles Matthew, Mark, Luke and John. It also includes the Acts of the Apostles.

(Letters and teachings that were passed on by word of mouth in the early Christian era, with emphasis on the letters of Paul) and the Apocalypse. The birth of Christianity is intertwined with the history of the Roman Empire and the history of the Jewish people. At its origin, Christianity was touted as a sect arising out of Judaism and terribly persecuted.

When Jesus Christ was born, around the year 4 BC, in the small city of Bethlehem, near Jerusalem, the Romans dominated Palestine. The Jews lived under the administration of Roman governors and, therefore, aspired for the arrival of the Messiah (they believed that he would be a great man of war and that he would rule politically) Named in the Torah (VT) as the envoy who would free them from Roman domination.

Until the age of 30, Jesus lived anonymously in Nazareth, a city located in the north of present-day Israel. At age 33 He would be crucified in Jerusalem and resurrect three days later. In a short time, approximately three years, he gathered followers (the 12 apostles) and toured the region preaching his doctrine performing miracles, such as raising dead people and healing the blind.

He soon became known to all and large crowds followed him, but to the Jewish religious authorities he was a blasphemer, as he called himself the Messiah. He lacked the looks and power to be the leader who would free the region from Roman domination. He just preached peace, love of neighbor. To the Romans he was a popular agitator.

After being arrested and killed, the tendency was for his followers to disperse and his teachings to be forgotten. The opposite happened. It is precisely on this fact that the Christian faith is based. As the prophets in the Old Testament had anticipated, Christ was resurrected, appeared to his apostles (Apostle means sent.) Who were hidden and ordered them to spread throughout the world preaching his message of love, peace, restoration and salvation?

Christianity established itself as a religion of divine origin. Its founder was the very son of God, sent as savior and builder of history together with man. To be a Christian, therefore, would be to engage in Christ's redemptive work, based on faith in his teachings. Quickly, Christian doctrine spread throughout the Mediterranean region and reached the heart of the Roman Empire. The spread of Christianity throughout Greece and Asia Minor was the work of the apostle Paul, who was not one of the 12 and would have been called to the mission by Jesus himself. Christian communities multiplied. Rivalries arose. In Rome, many Christians were turned into martyrs, eaten by lions at Colosseum spectacles, as targets for the wrath of emperors beset by corruption and debauchery.

The Church Through the Ages

Emperor Constantine converted to Christianity and granted freedom of worship, which facilitated the expansion of the doctrine throughout the empire. Before Constantine, meetings took place underground, the famous catacombs that can still be visited in Rome today.

Christianity, even asserting itself as of divine origin, is, like any religion, practiced by human beings. With freedom of thought and different ways of thinking. Deviations from course and historical situations determined the splits that divided Christianity into various confessions (the main ones being those of Catholics, Protestants and Orthodox).

The first major rift came in 1054, when the Patriarch of Constantinople, Michael Keroularios, broke with the pope, separating the so-called Orthodox Eastern Churches from Rome controlled by Rome. Byzantium and later Constantinople (today's Istanbul in Turkey) would be until 1453 the capital of the Eastern Roman Empire, or Byzantine Empire.

The Western Roman Empire had fallen long before, in 476, marking the beginning of the Middle Ages. And it was precisely in the so-called Middle Ages, still today one of the darkest periods in history, that Christianity faced its greatest challenges, producing successes and errors.

This journey culminated in the second great split, starting in 1517. The German theologian Martin Luther, a member of the Augustinian religious order, rebelled against the practice of selling indulgences and began to defend the thesis that man is only saved by faith.

Luther is excommunicated and founds the Lutheran Church. It does not recognize papal authority, denies the worship of saints and ends the mandatory confession and celibacy of priests and religious.

But he keeps the sacraments of baptism and the Eucharist. Later, the so-called Protestant Reformation gave rise to numerous other Christian churches, each with different interpretations of biblical passages or teachings of Christ. Others raised by the Holy Spirit, continue the purposes of the Lord God. Emperor Constantine converted to Christianity and granted freedom of worship, which facilitated the expansion of the doctrine throughout the empire. Before Constantine, meetings took place underground.

The famous catacombs that can still be visited in Rome today. Christianity, even asserting itself as of divine origin, is, like any religion, practiced by human beings. With freedom of thought and different ways of thinking. Deviations from course and historical situations determined the splits that divided Christianity into various confessions (the main ones being those of Catholics, Protestants and Orthodox).

The first major rift came in 1054, when the Patriarch of Constantinople, Michael Keroularios, broke with the pope. Separating from the Christianity controlled by Rome the Eastern churches, called orthodox. Byzantium and later Constantinople (today's Istanbul in Turkey) would be until 1453 the capital of the Eastern Roman Empire, or Byzantine Empire. The Western Roman Empire had fallen long before, in 476, marking the beginning of the Middle Ages.

And it was precisely in the so-called Middle Ages, still today one of the darkest periods in history, that Christianity faced its greatest challenges, producing successes and errors. This journey culminated in the second great split, starting in 1517. The German theologian Martin Luther, a member of the Augustinian religious order, rebelled against the practice of selling indulgences and began to defend the thesis that man is only saved by faith. Luther is excommunicated and founds the Lutheran Church. Does not recognize papal authority. It denies the worship of saints and ends the mandatory confession.

And celibacy of priests and religious. But he keeps the sacraments of baptism and the Eucharist. Later, the so-called Protestant Reformation gave rise to numerous other Christian churches, each with different interpretations of biblical passages or teachings of Christ. Others raised by the Holy Spirit, continue the purposes of the Lord God.

3.2 The Second Phase of the Christian Church

We can define as the second cycle of the church the period that goes from after the death of the apostles, during the persecution of Christianity that began with Emperor Nero in 67 A.D to Diocletian in 303 AD. Shortly after this long period of persecution and death to Christians in the first century, Roman Catholicism and its idolatrous doctrines were installed, after the supposed conversion of the current emperor and his position as the first supreme leader of the new religion. From that point in the history of the church, the doctrine of salvation, instituted by the Son of God and passed on to new converts from Christianity, was replaced by the idolatrous heresies of Roman Catholicism, where the true worship of God in spirit and truth (worship the Lord through faith, without the need to see him physically, and everywhere.

Not just inside a temple or before the altar) was replaced by the worship of idols (statues) of those who were part of the clergy after they died. After the death of the first leaders of the Jerusalem church, those who succeeded the ecclesiastical leadership did not have the same determination to keep the reins of the Christian faith and gave in to the emperors who assumed the religious power of the time. In other words: The church that had its foundations formed in the teachings of Christ in Jerusalem ceased to exist over the centuries, giving way to mysticism and the worship of Roman Catholic images. With such changes the erroneous form of worship lasted for centuries.

So much so that the true God was replaced by statues made of sticks or plaster. And the person of the emperor became a kind of being sacred and deserving of reverence. With this began, too, the revolt on the part of those who disagreed with the futile idea of being a natural man to demand to be adored, a clergy composed of priests, bishops and cardinals snubbing lusts.

Covered in gold and silver while seeing themselves as a common people, they lived on the margins of the walls of Rome. In complete misery and abandonment, forced to pay heavy taxes and without any right to know the truths taught by Christ and to gain free salvation through the sacrifice of the cross.

All of this created the foundations for the beginning of the Great Reformation, which gave rise to the third phase of the Christian church. It all started with Martin Luther's opposition to Catholic concepts that the pope would be the ultimate representative of the church and his doctrine of practicing idolatry.

"During the Middle Ages, the Catholic Church was the object of several movements that proposed to reform its structures, correcting abuses by the clergy and recovering the original purity of Christianity. However, all the authors of these reforms — popes, bishops, founders of religious orders — were always people belonging to the Church and incapable of leaving this institution, no matter how much they disagreed with it.

Anyway, they wanted to clean up the house and not build another one. At the end of the Middle Ages, however, religious discontents against the Church accumulated in such a way that they led to a movement of rupture:

The Reform

The reformists definitively broke with the Catholic Church, effectively breaking the unity of Western Christian thought.

The reform represented one of the fundamental historical movements that marked the beginning of modern times, being motivated by a complex set of causes that went beyond the limits of a mere religious contestation of the Catholic Church. This is because the man of the sixteenth century reflected, in terms of religion, a whole series of discontents that referred to his material living conditions, both on the political, social and economic levels.

The Main Causes of the Reform

There is a whole range of religious, socio-economic and political causes that help to understand the Reformation.

Religious Causes

A climate of critical reflection and spiritual unrest spread among many European Christians. With the use of the press, the number of copies of the Bible available to scholars increased. The dissemination of the Bible and other religious works contributed to the formation of a more personal desire to understand divine truths, without the intermediation of priests.

From this new spirit of interiorization and individualization of religion, which led to the free examination of the Scriptures, different interpretations of Christian doctrine emerged. In this sense, we can mention, for example, a religious current that, seeking support in the work of Saint Augustine, affirmed that man's salvation was only achieved through faith. These ideas were in opposition to the official position of the Church.

Based on St. Thomas Aquinas, by which man's salvation was achieved through faith and good works. Analyzing the behavior of the clergy, these Christians began to vigorously condemn a series of abuses and corruptions that were being practiced. The high clergy of Rome encouraged numerous businesses involving religion.

Such as the trade in the sacred relics of the thorns that crowned the forehead of Christ. The cloths that soaked the blood from your face, personal belongings of the Saints etc.). In addition to the trade in sacred relics, the Church began to sell indulgences, that is, the forgiveness of sins.

Thus, with a certain payment intended to finance the works of the Church, the faithful could buy their salvation. On the moral plane, the situation of countless members of the Church was also deplorable, being the object of several criticisms.

The cases of priests involved in romantic scandals, of monks who lived drunk as vagabonds, and of bishops who only accumulated personal wealth, sold the sacraments and cared little for religion, multiplied.

Socioeconomic Causes

The theological conception of the church, developed during the Medieval Period, was adapted to the feudal system, which was based on the closed economy and the self-sufficiency of the manors.

Where commerce subsisted only as a marginal activity. Therefore, traditional Catholic theology condemned the obtaining of excessive profit, of usury, in commercial operations.

Defending the practice of fair pricing. With the beginning of modern times, maritime and commercial expansion developed, and within this new context the economic morality of the Church began to clash with the activity of the big bourgeoisie.

This class, committed to developing commercial activities to the fullest, felt uncomfortable with the traditional conceptions of the Church, which branded the impetuous pursuit of profit a sin. Thus, this bourgeoisie began to feel the need for a new religious ethic, more suited to the spirit of commercial capitalism.

This ideological need of the bourgeoisie was largely satisfied with the Protestant ethic, which would emerge with the Reformation. It should be noted, however, that not all reformist leaders were willing to encourage the practices of capitalism. This is the case, for example, of Luther, who severely condemned luxury and usury, proposing for Christians an ideal of modest life, in which anxiety for profit and vanity for material wealth would not exist.

Political Causes

The 16th century was a period of strengthening of national monarchies. The Catholic Church, based in Rome and speaking Latin, presented itself as an institution of universal character, being a factor of unity in the Christian world.

These notions, however, lost force as national sentiments developed with great vigor. Each state, with its monarchy, its language, its people and its traditions, was more interested in self-assertion as a nation than in being part of a Christendom obedient to the Church. Opposing the papacy and the centralizing command of the Catholic Church, the Religious Reformation met nationalist concerns, allowing the autonomy of national Churches.

Martin Luther's Reformation

Martin Luther (1483-1546) was born in Eisleben, Saxony, the son of a mining contractor who achieved some economic prosperity. Influenced by his father, he entered the University of Erfurt in 1501 to study law, but his temperament inclined him to religious life. In 1505.

After nearly dying in a violent storm, he joined the Order of Augustinian Monks, fulfilling a promise made to St. Anne. A serious, methodical, and diligent scholar, Luther gained intellectual prestige, becoming, in 1508, a professor at the University of Wittenberg.

In 1510 he traveled to Rome, from where he returned disappointed by the climate of corruption he had sensed among the high clergy. In the years 1511 to 1513, he deepened his theological studies, until the ideas for the creation of a new religious doctrine began to mature in his spirit.

In the epistles of St. Paul, he found a phrase that seemed fundamental to him: "the just shall be saved by faith". Luther concluded that man, corrupted by original sin, could only be saved by unconditional faith in God.

Faith alone, and not deeds done, would be the only instrument capable of justifying sins and leading to salvation, thanks to divine mercy. In 1517, the incident broke out that would provoke the split between Luther and the Catholic Church.

Revolving around the episode known as the sale of indulgences. With the objective of raising funds to finance the reconstruction of St. Peter's Basilica, Pope Leo X allowed indulgences (pardon for sins) to be granted to all the faithful who contributed financially to the Church.

Scandalized by this salvation bought with money, Luther posted on the door of the Church of Wittenberg a public manifesto (the 95 theses), in which he protested against the Pope's attitude and expounded the elements of his doctrine. Then began a long discussion.

Between Luther and the ecclesiastical authorities, culminating in his excommunication by the Pope in 1520. Showing contempt and revolt before the Church, Luther burned the Papal bull Exsurge domine, which condemned him, in a public square.

The Lutheran Doctrine

Let us briefly see a summary of the main points of Lutheran doctrine: Church: proclaimed the creation of autonomous national Churches.

Religious work could be done by people not obligated to priestly celibacy (obligation to marry). Luther accepted the dependence of the Church on the State. The language of religious ceremonies should be that of each nation and not Latin, which was the official language of Catholic ceremonies.

Religious Rite: the religious ceremony should obey simpler rites, reducing the pomp existing in Catholic cults. Saints and images were abolished.

Holy Book: The Bible was the holy book of Lutheranism, representing the only source of faith. Its reading and interpretation should be done by all Christians. Luther, in 1534, translated a Greek original of the Bible into German.

Human Salvation: Man is saved by faith in God.

And not for the works he does. Sacraments were preserved as basic sacraments baptism and the Eucharist.

The Expansion of Lutheranism

Alongside the purely religious problems, there were a number of social and economic factors that favored the spread of Luther's ideas in Germany. Among them, the fact that a large part of German lands belongs to the Catholic Church stands out, with great interest from the nobility in taking possession of these lands.

At that time, what we call Germany was nothing more than a set of principalities and autonomous cities, not having, therefore, a unified country, with authentic political unity. The region was part of the domains of the Holy Roman Empire, controlled by the Habsburg Dynasty, whose emperor was in Spain. The emperor was an ally of the Pope and sought, in this way, to preserve a certain unity and power over the German princes. Thirsty for power and wealth, the upper classes (nobility and bourgeoisie) were discontented with the Church and with the emperor's command.

On the other hand, the less favored social classes (peasants and urban artisans) also blamed the Church for the situation of misery and exploitation to which they were victims.

There was, therefore, a certain consensus among the different social classes against the Church. Led by Thomas Münzer, the peasants, from 1524 onwards, organized a series of revolts against rich and noble priests, owners of large land holdings. Violently, peasants fought for land ownership and an end to exploitation. The ruling classes then united to quell the peasant revolt, with the support of Luther, who published a manifesto whose title bore the words:

"Against the murderous and thieving peasant gangs...".

Clashes with the powerful, the peasants were crushed: more than a hundred thousand died and the leader Thomas Munzer. was beheaded. In exchange for his support of the ruling classes, Luther found powerful allies between the nobility and the upper bourgeoisie.

That helped him to spread his religious doctrine throughout northern Germany, Sweden, Denmark and Norway. It was these allies who, in 1529, protested against the preservation of the measures taken by the emperor against Luther, which prevented each state from adopting its own religion. It was from this protest that the name Protestant was spread to designate non-Catholic Christians.

Not being heard by the emperor, the group of leading Protestants formed, in 1531, a political-military league (League of Smalkalde) To fight against the Catholic forces linked to Emperor Charles V. Only in 1555 did the emperor accept the official existence of the Lutheran Churches, signing the Peace of Augsburg with the Protestants. It was the final legal recognition of the religious separation from the Christian world.

Calvin's Reformation

John Calvin (1509 - 1564) was born in Noyon, France, and developed his studies in Theology and Law in that country. Influenced by Guillaume Farel, he adhered to Protestant ideas.

When, in 1534, the French Catholic authorities began to pursue those suspected of r heresies, Calvin fled to Switzerland, where the reform movement had already begun, under the leadership of Ulrich Zwingli (1484-1531).

In his preaching's, Zwingli gave greater importance than Luther to the belief in the predestination of men for salvation, putting less value on the aspect of justification by faith.

With his rationalist spirit, Zwingli won the support of the Swiss merchant bourgeoisie, who admired the objectivity of his actions and the practical side of his ideas. His religious work prepared the way for the ideas of John Calvin to develop there. In 1536, Calvin published his main work.

 The Institution of the Christian Religion, in which he affirmed that the human being was absolutely predestined to deserve Heaven. Or Hell. Calvin explained that, through Adam's fault, all men were born sinners (original sin), but God had chosen some people to be saved, while others would be condemned to eternal damnation.

Therefore, nothing that men could do in life could alter their destiny, which had already been outlined. Faith, existing in some people, could be interpreted as a sign that they belonged to the group of those chosen by God for salvation. Such people, the elect, would feel within their hearts an irresistible desire to fight the evil that populates the world, simply for the glory of God. The economic prosperity of some people, their material wealth.

Also came to be interpreted by Calvin's followers as a sign of predestined salvation. In 1538, Calvin was expelled from Switzerland, due to his excesses of rigor and authoritarianism. However, he managed to return in 1541 and consolidated his power in the city of Geneva, becoming absolute master of the Government and the new Calvinist Church, until the year 1561.

During this period, Geneva lived a theocratic regime, in which religious and political principles were confused. Among the bodies created by the Calvinist government, the Consistory stood out, in charge of the moral vigilance of citizens and requesting punishment from the State. Among the attitudes condemned by Calvinism are cited. For example, gambling, image worship, dancing, adultery and heresy.

With the penalties imposed on offenders varying according to the seriousness of the crime. Many were sentenced to death, including the physician Michael of Servetus, who was burned alive for denying original sin. Based on Calvinism, an ideal model of man, religious and worker was created, for whom economic success and the conquest of wealth were a sign of divine predestination to Paradise.

This ideology was very well accepted by the mercantile bourgeoisie, as its greed for profit was justified by religious ethics. Identifying itself with the bourgeoisie, Calvinism spread to various regions of Europe, such as France, England, Scotland and Holland – countries where commercial capitalism was expanding.

The Anglican Reformation

Henry VIII (1509-1547), King of England, had for a time been a faithful ally of the Pope, receiving from him the title of "Defender of the Faith". However, a series of political and economic factors also led Henry VIII to break with the Catholic Church and found a national Church in England, that is, the Anglican Church.

Among the main factors that provoked the Anglican Reform, we can highlight the following: * Strengthening the monarchy: The Catholic Church exerted great political influence within England, as it owned much of the land and monopolized the trade in sacred objects. To strengthen the power of the English monarchy, Henry VIII would have to reduce the Pope's influence within England; * Ownership of Church lands:

The English capitalist nobility had great economic interest in seizing Church lands. For this to happen it was necessary to unite around the king, so that the powers of the Catholic Church were weakened. King Henry VIII's petition for divorce: Married to the Spanish Princess Catherine of Aragon, Henry VIII had a daughter with her to succeed him on the throne.

However, the king was quite unhappy with his marriage. First, because of his wife's Spanish origins, as Spain was England's enemy. Second, because the king wanted a male heir and intended to marry Anne Boleyn. So, in 1529 he asked the Pope to annul his marriage to Catherine of Aragon, but he was met with the Supreme Pontiff's refusal.

Despite this, Henry VIII managed to get the English high clergy and Parliament to recognize the validity of his intentions. In 1534, the English Parliament voted an Act of Supremacy, by which it considered Henry VIII the supreme head of the Anglican National Church. "The English, by oath, must submit to this supremacy, otherwise they would be excommunicated and persecuted by royal justice. There was little resistance, including that of Thomas Moros, who was beheaded. The regular clergy was suppressed and their goods, returned to the crown, were sold". After the creation of the Anglican Church, with the successors of Henry VIII, a series of internal religious struggles arose. First, there was an attempt to implant, in the government of Edward VI (1547-1553), Calvinism in the country.

Then, in the government of Maria Tudor (1553-1558), daughter of Catherine of Aragon, there was a Catholic reaction. It was only during the government of Elisabeth I (1558-1603) that the Anglican Church was consolidated, which remains dominant in the country to this day.

Puritan Calvinism has, however, gained a large number of adherents among the bourgeoisie, however, a large number of adherents among the manufacturing bourgeoisie. It was from the Puritans that the great leaders of the 17th century English Revolution emerged.

The Form and Content of the Anglican Reform

The Anglican Church sought to develop an original reconciliation between the traditional rite of Catholicism and Protestant dogma.

In other words, the Catholic form was maintained in the ceremonies (conservation of the Catholic liturgy, of the ecclesiastical hierarchy, etc.)

And elements of the Protestant content were introduced into the doctrine (salvation by faith, preservation of only two sacraments - baptism and communion, etc.).

This was the solution found by the English monarchy to favor, in the country, the social coexistence of different rival religious groups.

Thus, according to the historical circumstances of each moment, the English monarchy directed the Anglican Church to emphasize the Catholic form or the Protestant content.

If he wanted to please Protestants, he valued the content of the services; if he wanted to please Catholics, he valued the formal rite of ceremonies.

The Catholic Reformation
Or Counter Reformation

In the face of Protestant movements, the initial and immediate reaction of the Catholic Church was to punish the rebel leaders, in the hope that the ideas of the reformers would not spread and the Christian world would regain its lost unity. This tactic, however, did not work as the Protestant movement advanced across Europe.

Gaining growing number of followers. It was therefore necessary to recognize the Protestant rupture. As a result, a broad movement to moralize the clergy and reorganize the Church's administrative structures gained strength within Catholicism. This movement to reform the Catholic Church became known as the Catholic Reformation or Counter Reformation. Its main leaders were Popes Paul III (1534-1549, Paul IV (1555-1559), Pius V (1566-1572) and Schist V (1585-1590). Reform, with a view to halting the advance of Protestantism. Among these measures, the following stand out:

Approval of the Jesuit Order: in the year 1540

Pope Paul III approved the creation of the Jesuit Order or Society of Jesus. It had been founded by the Spanish military Ignatius Loyola in 1534. Drawing inspiration from the military structure, the Jesuits considered themselves the soldiers of the Church, its elite troop, whose mission was to combat the expansion of Protestantism. However, combat had to be fought with the weapons of the spirit, and for this Ignatius of Loyola wrote a basic book, called

Spiritual exercises, in which it was proposed to program the individual's conversion to Catholicism, through contemplation techniques. The creation of religious schools was one of the main instruments of the Jesuits' strategy.

Another weapon used was non-Christian catechesis, that is, the Jesuits were committed to converting the peoples of the newly discovered continents to Catholicism. The aim was to expand Catholic rule to other continents.

* Convocation of the Council of Trent:

In the year 1545, Pope Paul III called a council, whose first meetings were held in the city of Trento, Italy. At the end of long years of work, ending in 1563, the Council presented a set of decisions designed to guarantee the unity of the Catholic faith and ecclesiastical discipline. Reacting to Protestant ideas, the Council of Trent reaffirmed several points of Catholic doctrine, such as:

1 - Human Salvation: depends on faith and good human works. The doctrine of predestination was therefore rejected;

2 - Source of Faith: religious dogma has the Bible as its source, and it is up to the Church to give it the correct interpretation

3 Religious Tradition — preserved by the Church and handed down to new generations. The Pope reaffirmed his position as successor of Peter, to whom Jesus Christ entrusted the construction of his Church; — The Mass and the presence of Christ: The Church reaffirmed that in the act of the Eucharist the real presence of Jesus in the bread and wine took place. this real presence of Christ was rejected by Protestants. The Council of Trent also determined the elaboration of a catechism with the fundamental points of Catholic doctrine. The creation of seminaries for the formation of priests and the maintenance of priestly celibacy;

* Reinstatement for the Inquisition:

In the year 1231 the Catholic Church created the Courts of Inquisition, which, over time, reduced its activities in several countries. However, with the advance of Protestantism, the Church decided to reactivate, in the middle of the 17th century.

The functioning of the Inquisition, which took charge, for example, of organizing a list of books prohibited to Catholics, the Index librorum prohibitorum. One of the first lists of banned books was published in 1564. The Message of Reform for Today — *Free Undergraduate Course – Bachelor's Degree Discipline: Ecclesiastical Law FIC SERVIÇOS EDUCACIONAIS LTDA*

3.3 The Third Stage of the Church (Religious Relativism)

As we read the history of the church and observe its trajectory from the beginnings until today, we observe how great the battle was waged by our precursors for the Gospel to reach the present day, with all the freedom we have to be able to spread it to the nations in around the earth. However, it would be naive of us to believe in the possibility of the existence of an inherent faith in Christ.

On the part of his followers in this modern world. No, we may have won the victory over the opponents of Christianity, who tried in every way to prevent the expansion of our teacher's teachings by prohibiting the reading of the Bible to his faithful, the martyrdom of ancient Christians by the Roman emperors in the cradle of church and persecution during the Protestant Counter Reformation in the 14th century. But without a doubt, we have arrived at the present time with an intense difference in the concepts and ideologies of the old way of believing and living the Christian doctrine that we were once taught.

2. Modernism and Religious Relativism

Modernity extended to all social fields and reached the pulpits of evangelical churches, where it considerably affected their doctrines. Concerning Christian ethics, which in the past made them inverse to the customs of other religions and identified its members as true opponents of pagan worldliness.

That is, those who did not know or did not accept the dictates of the Gospel preached by Jesus Christ. And left to his disciples, as a rule for those who wished to attain salvation and the guarantee of eternal life. And, along with these new concepts, the modernist tendencies to present God to man also emerged. If before, when the preaching model was based on the teaching left to us by Christ and his apostles, now preachers use false prophecies to attract spectators to the temples, which are always crowded in search of solutions to their many financial problems.

Promising false changes in the complicated lives of these people, they sell cures and miracles to a people who almost always seek material results and do not care for the salvation of the soul.

Which should be the priority of those who seek Jesus and his Gospel. With the emergence of the "Doctrine of Prosperity", created and spread by the Neo-Pentecostals, few still take the trouble to go to the temple in order to pray to God, as a form of reverence and adoration. The general objective is to consult the specialists in "prophecies" to find out if they will be "blessed" and what is the amount to be paid so that the windows of heaven are opened and blessings showered upon each one of them.

The religious mania of this Christian Era is to market the gifts of the Spirit of God, left to freely benefit the church. They sell prophecies, cures, miracles and even false guesses. This is the pitiful spiritual state of the modern Christian. In fact, we have already gone beyond modernism and are living in religious relativism, a period in Christian history where everyone thinks only about themselves and their basic consumption needs. Give greater priority to the material and disregard for the spiritual. The old idea of "loving your neighbor as yourself" and sharing your goods with your neighbor has fallen by the wayside and selfishness is what prevails in social relations, even in communities declared to be Christian.

The church, as a community planted and immersed in its historical time, suffers the consequences of this relativism. One of the greatest evidences of the influence of relativism in the contemporary church is its tendency towards ecumenism. The defense of the indiscriminate acceptance of any and all beliefs reveals how the exclusivist character of the gospel sounds bad to contemporary ears.

Another feature that has become increasingly common within the church is the questioning of the need for and absence of church discipline. This practice reveals that not only relativism regarding knowledge has entered the church, but also ethical-moral relativism. (Gene 2013: 8) Followers of this current religious trend no longer cling to the biblical promises, seen as outdated.

That God will supply their needs and that they should not be worried about tomorrow, suggested by Jesus in the Gospels. And they run in search of a way to accelerate divine attention to their most urgent needs, even if they have to pay dearly for the intercessory service of such a prophet. And who will dare to condemn the ambitious and detached attitude of the current relativist "Christians"? Not even the most conservative leaders dare to oppose his views that if God is the owner of gold and silver, his children cannot live in intense poverty.

This rather complex theory (relativism) can be seen in the everyday words and actions of people in our time. Probably most readers can already see how much contemporary man cares about his history individually, as if it were not related to history in general. Probably, most readers of this text have already had a discussion closed with the following words: "It's not worth discussing. After all, you have your truth and I have mine". Or, who has never been asked rhetorically, after having issued a value judgment about something or someone: "who are you to judge?". These words and actions reveal how relativism has taken hold of our day. (Gene 2013: 9).

In short: to be a Christian in our day is to receive rich blessings from heaven, and the correct church or religion is the one that preaches, teaches and provides these things.

3. The Social Consequences of Relativism

3.1 The Last Days Apostasy

Paul, apostle of the Lord Jesus Christ, guiding his faithful disciple, Timothy. A young pastor who started his activities as a leader of one of the newly founded churches. He warned him about the revelations God had given him regarding the apostasy. How she would take care of the church in the last days and how far Christians would distance themselves from biblical teachings, prompting him to preach the truths of Christ while they wanted to hear them (1 Timothy 4:1-5)

And this time has come, most Christians of this century have already become apostates from the faith.

This is, without a doubt, one more consequence of man's distancing from God, of the loss of the church's commitment to its primordial mission of not only announcing, but faithfully living the Gospel. For she was called to be the light of this dark world, the salt of the earth (Matthew 5:13-16).

And, by losing this quality, the world is lost in the densest spiritual darkness. The church is summed up in its members in particular, in each believer, each disciple of Jesus. Not in the temple made of wood or bricks, nor in a particular religious flag.

And it is from each of those who one day confessed to believing the Gospel message and went down to the waters during baptism, receiving forgiveness for their many sins, being cleansed by the blood of the Lamb. And they committed themselves to the "go" of Jesus to preach the Good News of Salvation to every creature, to the ends of the earth.

Whom will God charge for the neglect of not having brought the news to sinners that there is a way out of their pain and frustration? dilemmas and sufferings. Letting the wicked continue to practice wickedness, and the unclean commit even more immoralities, to the point where the dense spiritual darkness of the world has come to the state in which it has arrived. If the church becomes inert and does not release its glow, if its light is dimmed under a bushel, the earth will be filled with the blood that violence will spread over it. The mission of the church is to spread love and peace on earth through the preaching of the Gospel. If this were done today, according to God's purpose.

And as it was the early work of the early Christians, certainly the rate of violence would be much lower, as the hearts of most people would be filled with mercy and not hate. But unfortunately, the church fails in its mission to sow the good seed and because it does not want to sacrifice itself for humanity, as Jesus did. Assuming that the meaning of mission in the biblical context begins with the revelation of God himself in history. It soon becomes clear that the paradigm for any definition of the term "ecclesiological mission" must be understood through the mission of God himself. Since, both in the old and in the new covenant, we can have access to the modus operandi of the divine mission in relation to the rescue of humanity, it is valid to learn from God himself the meaning of mission:

Mission is personal delivery.

Mission is personal renunciation.

mission is to evangelize

Mission is to lead souls to Christ

Mission is to fight evil (sin)

Mission for the church is to fully fulfill the idea of Jesus"

4 – THE FUTURE OF THE CHURCH

There is a promise made for the New Jerusalem of God, the one that will safely dwell in a special future that the Lord has already reserved for her since the foundation of the world, it is described in several biblical passages, especially in the books of Revelation and Isaiah. Both he and John were privileged to be able to contemplate the future that will be reserved for those who manage to remain faithful to the end.

Those two seers had the honor to see, in advance, the glory of God's people after they pass the evil days that put the earth in deep darkness. After all the suffering, anguish and persecution that the Bride of Christ goes through in this world, there will be a reward without measure at the end of the journey, for she will be exalted and her radiance without comparison.

The effects of human wickedness will no longer be seen, for death has been conquered and sin was torn from the earth, Satan destroyed and hell undone. Only the light of God will illuminate the Holy City and its inhabitants, peace will be eternal and Christians will finally find their deserved rest. Thus, tells us the Scriptures: "Arise, shine, for your light is coming, and the glory of the LORD is rising upon you; for, behold, darkness covered the earth, and darkness covered the peoples; but upon thee the Lord will come appearing, and his glory will be seen upon thee. And the Gentiles will walk in your light, and kings in the brightness that is born to you. Lift up your eyes round about, and see; all these have already gathered together, and come unto thee; your sons will come from afar.

And your daughters will be brought up by your side. Then you will see it, and you will be enlightened, and your heart will tremble and be enlarged". (Isaiah 60:1) This certainty of a new life in complete peace in the presence of God, resting from all your labors and rejoicing in the victory gained after so many pains and sufferings in the course of your walk in this world.

It will be the reward for the patience with which the redeemed of Christ endured everything before their oppressors without, however, backing down. The angel was very clear in the revelation he made to John on the Isle of Patmos, in the revelation of the Apocalypse, in stating that cowards will not enter the kingdom of Christ.

Heavenly mansions are reserved for those who have not refused to give even their lives for the sake of the Gospel. Who loved more the hope of living eternally with their Savior than being able to enjoy the momentary comfort of rich palaces or the support of the mortal kings of this world?

Knowing and believing that in the life to come they would be immensely honored by the one who guaranteed them the glory of immortality:

"Sing joyfully, O barren one, who gave no birth; break into song, and exclaim with joy, you who had no birth pains? For more are the children of the lonely woman than the children of the married woman, saith the LORD.

Enlarge the place of your tent, and let the curtains of your dwellings be extended; do not hinder him, lengthen your cords, and secure your stakes.

Because you will overflow to the right and to the left; and thy seed shall possess the Gentiles, and cause the desolate cities to be inhabited. Fear not, because you will not be ashamed. And do not be ashamed, for you will not be humiliated.

but you will forget the shame of your youth, and you will no longer remember the reproach of your widowhood. For your Creator is your husband.

The Lord of hosts is his name; and the Holy One of Israel is your Redeemer; that he is called the God of all the earth. For the Lord called thee as a helpless woman sad in spirit; as the woman of youth, who was despised, says your God. For a brief moment I left you, but with great mercies I will collect you.

With a little wrath I hid my face from you for a moment; but with everlasting kindness I will have compassion on you, says the Lord your Redeemer. For this will be to me as the waters of Noah; for I swore that the waters of Noah would no more pass over the earth; so I have sworn that I will no longer be angry with you, neither will I rebuke you. For the mountains will withdraw, and the hills will be shaken; but my kindness will not depart from you. And the covenant of my peace will not change, says the Lord who has compassion on you. Thou oppressed, hurled with the tempest, and disconsolate, behold, I will lay thy stones with every ornament.

 And I will be found you on the sapphires. And I will make thy stained-glass windows with rubies, and thy doors with carbuncles, and all thy stones with pleasant stones. And all your children shall be taught of the Lord; and the peace of your children will be abundant. In justice you will be established; you will be far from oppression, because you will no longer fear; and also of terror, because it will not come to you. Behold, they will surely come to join against you, but it will not be for me; whoever gathers against thee will fall because of thee.

Behold, I created the blacksmith, who blows the coals into the fire, and who produces the tool for his work; I also created the devastator, to destroy. Every tool prepared against thee shall not prosper, and every tongue that rises up against thee in judgment thou shalt condemn it; this is the inheritance of the servants of the Lord, and their righteousness from me". (Isaiah 54:1-17) We, all Christians who strive to remain faithful to God in carrying out his ordinances. will eventually come to behold his face on that long-awaited day of complete redemption.

We symbolize your church, your Bride, elected the heir of the right to enter your Kingdom through the doors (Revelation 22:14) It is not about temples built by human hands, nor plates of this or that religious denomination, but of each one in private. That in fact is firm in the certainty of his coming. The Lord's chosen ones will be gathered together by his angels from the four corners of the earth (Revelation 14:14,15)

And they will be brought to the presence of the bridegroom who will receive them on high under the glory that is deserved. This message must be proclaimed day and night to the faithful of the earth so that their weary hands and knees do not faint, nor fail to believe in the fulfillment of these divine promises that will certainly not fail. "And I saw a new heaven, and a new earth. Because the first heaven and the first earth have passed away, and the sea no longer exists.

And I, John, saw the Holy City, the new Jerusalem, descending from God from God, adorned like a wife dressed for her husband. And I heard a great voice from heaven, saying, Behold the tabernacle of God with men, for he shall dwell with them, and they shall be his people, and the same God shall be with them, and shall be their God.

And God will wipe away every tear from their eyes; and there will be no more death, no more crying, no more crying, no more pain; because the first things are already passed. And he that sat upon the throne said: Behold, I make all things new. And he said to me: Write; because these words are true and faithful. And he told me more: It is fulfilled. I am Alpha and Omega, the beginning and the end. To whoever is thirsty, I will freely give him from the fountain of the water of life. Whoever wins will inherit all things; and I will be his God, and he will be my son. But as for the timid, and the unbelievers, and the abominable, and the murderers, and the harlots, and the sorcerers, and the idolaters, and all liars.

CONCLUSION

The church of Christ had its beginning from the moment he started to select his first disciples and commissioned them to go preach the gospel to every creature (Mark 16:15), its foundations were laid definitively after his death and resurrection, when ascended into heaven and commanded them to expect to receive power from heaven and, soon thereafter, to carry the good news of redemption to the ends of the earth (Acts 1:8) and for over two thousand centuries it has fully fulfilled its mission of announce to the lost that the solution for mankind is found in Jesus Christ, the one who gave his life on a rough cross so that whoever believes in him may not perish, but have eternal life (John

REFERENCES

MARK DISCROLL. Sexual Sin. Private Hermeneutics, Synopsis, São Paulo, 2010.

MILLARD J. ERICKSON. Systematic Theology — LEE, CARLOS - Learning from the Scriptures, 2011

GOSPEL MORE. God's Letter — The Importance of Christian Witness, part 1, 2011

PRUDENT WORD. Bible, Definition of Doctrine, volume-1, chapter 17 the Faithfulness of God, 2015

PORTAL BIBLEINFO.COM. The Second Coming of Jesus, 2012

FIC SERVIÇOS EDUCACIONAIS LTDA www.fic.vcx.com.br

BIBLE PERSONAL APPLICATION. Commentary on Pedro, CPAD, Rio de Janeiro, p1761. 2004

FIC. Educational Services, Undergraduate Course. 2017